ELVIS

ELVIS

Sandra Forty

T&J

Published by TAJ Books International LLC 2013

219 Great Lake Drive,

Cary, North Carolina, USA

27519

www.tajbooks.com

All notations of errors or omissions (author inquiries, permissions) concerning the content of this book should be addressed to

info@tajbooks.com.

ISBN 978-1-84406-273-7

Printed in China.

1 2 3 4 5 17 16 15 14 13

Our thanks also to wonderful picture archives of SuperStock.com.

Acknowledgments

Elvis has a fantastic fan base and a plethora of books, magazines, and websites devoted to his personality and his talent. In particular, the following are recommended:

http://www.elvis.com/
http://www.elvispresleymusic.com.au
http://www.elvisrecords.us/
http://scottymoore.net/
http://www.elvis-history-blog.com/
http://elvis-presleys-kingdom.com/

Specific acknowledgements:
Circle G
http://circlegfoundation.co.uk/?page_id=45

Karate
http://www.tracyskarate.com/Stories/was_elvis_really_a_black_belt.htm

Memphis homes
http://memphis.about.com/od/elvispresley/ss/elvishomes2.htm

CONTENTS

EARLY YEARS

Elvis is one of the great icons of modern popular culture, a man whose image has become part of the day-to-day world and whose contributions to music and style have transcended the boundaries of color, country, and creed.

It's almost impossible to measure his contribution to modern music. He arrived at the birth of rock 'n' roll and gave it a raw sensuality that has continued to today. Alarmed by his stage presence, the establishment—the church, the law, the press, and TV—overreacted, lambasting his music, his singing ability, and his style. But they could not diminish the overwhelming fascination that greeted his every move and the selling power that his performances generated. There had been others before him who had captured the youth market—Frank Sinatra was the most obvious—but none did so at such a crucial cultural turning point. The post-war baby boomers took Elvis and rock 'n' roll to their hearts and redefined popular music, preparing the ground for the explosion of styles in the 1960s.

Influenced by country music, gospel music, and rhythm and blues—particularly the black music of Memphis and the Mississippi delta—Elvis blended the sounds into a unique modern style that broke down racial barriers and ultimately created a legend that would not fade with death. Helped by charm, humor, sensational good looks, and a voice in a million, he appealed to people all over the world. His death in 1977 led to heartbreak that knew no boundaries.

Elvis did more to promote American culture and style around the globe than almost any other figure. In his 20-odd years as a top-flight entertainer, he became the top-selling solo artist of all time with over a billion sales from 600 recordings, 70 albums (20 reaching #1 on the charts, and to date 90 have gone gold, 52 platinum, and 25 multi-platinum), 30 EPs, and over a hundred singles, 33 of which made #1. On top of this, he served for two years in the U.S. Army, made 33 dramatic films, and performed many times live in front of ground-breaking audiences.

A young Elvis with his mother Gladys (above) and 2-year-old Elvis with mother Gladys and father Vernon (right)

Elvis Presley's birthplace in Tupelo, Mississippi

EARLY YEARS

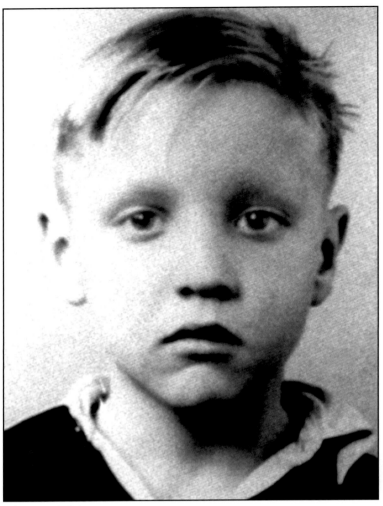

A young Elvis

Elvis in 1943

A teen-aged Elvis Presley (second from left) with friends Farley Guy, Paul Dougher, and Buzzy Forbess

EARLY YEARS

It is almost impossible to do justice to Elvis' talent in a book. The following is just a bare bones account of his life and his work.

1933

June 7: Vernon Elvis Presley marries Gladys Love Smith at the Assembly of God Church—where they had met—in Tupelo, Mississippi.

1934

Vernon, with help from his father, Jessie, who lived next door, and his brother, Vester, build a typical Southern "shotgun" shack. They can't afford electricity and there's no indoor plumbing.

1935

January 8: At 4:35 a.m., at home, Gladys Love Presley gives birth to two sons. The first, Jessie Garon, is stillborn. The second is healthy and is named Elvis Aaron.

1938

May 25: Odd-job man Vernon—along with Gladys' brother Travis—is sentenced to three years in Parchman Penitentiary for forgery. During this period the family loses their house and starts renting.

1939

February 6: Vernon is released and finds work with the WPA at the shipyards of Pascagoula, Mississippi.

1941

September: Elvis starts school at the East Tupelo Consolidated School.

1945

October 3: Encouraged by his class teacher, Mrs. Oleta Grimes, and the school's principal, Mr. Cole, Elvis sings "Old Shep" at the talent contest of the 38th Annual Mississippi-Alabama Fair and Dairy Show in Tupelo, which is broadcast on Tupelo's radio station, WELO Radio.

1946

January 8: Elvis receives his first guitar on his 11th birthday.

September: Elvis starts 6th grade at Milam Junior High School. He regularly brings his guitar to school and plays during lunch breaks.

Elvis in 1959

Jerry Lee Lewis, Carl Perkins, Elvis Presley, and Johnny Cash: The Million Dollar Quartet, 1956

EARLY YEARS

1947

Elvis becomes friendly with Mississippi Slim—who has a show on WELO—through Slim's younger brother, who is in the same class as Elvis. Slim helps Elvis' technique and sets up his first radio performance.

1948

November 6: Elvis says goodbye to Tupelo, singing "Leaf on a Tree" in farewell to his class. The family moves to Memphis, Tennessee, in search of a better life. Elvis enrolls at L.C. Humes High School and the family attends the Assembly of God Church.

1949

September 20: The family rents a two-bedroom public housing apartment in Lauderdale Courts. Elvis' time at L.C. Humes is tough; his music teacher doesn't approve of his singing style and gives him a grade of C. Elvis, with his long hair and sideburns, is viewed as an outsider, something enhanced by his love of what is seen as "black" music—gospel and rhythm and blues.

1950

After practicing with a neighbor—Jesse Lee Denson—Elvis, Denson, and the Burnette brothers (Dorsey and Johnny) start playing together.

1952

The Presley family's income rises above the allowable limit for the public housing project so they have to move, ending up in an apartment opposite their previous apartment at Lauderdale Courts.

1953

April: Elvis competes in his school's annual Minstrel Show and his performance wins over many of his contemporaries who had hitherto thought him a rather strange, reclusive figure.

June 3: Elvis graduates and starts his first full-time job at the Precision Tool Company.

Wanda Jackson and Elvis, 1955

Johnny Cash and Elvis Presley, 1956

22

July/August: Elvis goes to the Memphis Recording Studio—later called Sun Studios—set up by Sam Phillips in 1950 at 706 Union Avenue. Phillips set up the Sun Records label in 1952. For a cost of $3.98, Elvis records an acetate demo of "My Happiness" and "That's When Your Heartache Begins," which he later gives to his mother as a belated birthday present. The session is handled by Phillips' assistant, Marion Keisker. Elvis' motivation for using this studio rather than other cheaper options was probably in the hope that Phillips—who had already made a name for himself in the music industry—would further his career. Nothing comes of his first recording although the only surviving acetate is valued today, unsurprisingly, in millions of dollars.

1954

January 4: Elvis makes another acetate demo—"I'll Never Stand in Your Way" and "It Wouldn't Be the Same Without You," this time with Sam Phillips. Again there is no immediate response, but he keeps the contact going, regularly showing his face at 706 Union Avenue.

January 30: Elvis meets Dixie Locke, whom he will date into 1955.

April 20: Elvis starts work as a driver at Crown Electric.

May 15: Elvis endures his second audition for a local band ... and his second rejection. The first was for the Songfellows, who didn't think he could sing harmonies; the second was for Eddie Bond.

June 26: Elvis' persistence pays off when Sam Phillips contacts him to try out a song he has received—"Without You." The recording is unremarkable, but Phillips suggests he team up with guitarist Scotty Moore. Elvis visits Scotty straight away and he introduces Elvis to bassist Bill Black.

July 5: Today, Elvis discovers his unique sound.

Dixie Locke and Elvis, 1955

EARLY CAREER

KWKH's

Louisiana Hayride

With a cast of
more than 40 radio
and recording
stars including

SLIM WHITMAN
JIM REEVES
ELVIS PRESLEY
JOHNNY WALKER
JIMMY NEWMAN
and many others
3½-Hour Stage Show
and Radio Broadcast

**HEART O' TEXAS
COLISEUM**

TONIGHT
8:00 — 11:30 P. M.

ELVIS PRESLEY

Adults $1.00   Children 50c

Tickets on Sale At

THE COFFEE CUP
6TH AND AUSTIN

Elvis Presley and the singing group The Browns, which performed with Elvis at The Louisiana Hayride

A 1954 original, hand-painted concert poster for a performance at the Eagles Nest in Memphis

EAGLES NEST

IN PERSON

MEMPHIS OWN...

ELVIS PRESLEY

WITH SCOTTY & BILL

♪ SINGING ♪♪

"HEART BREAKER" *"THATS ALL RIGHT"* *

* *"GOOD ROCKIN"* *

I Spent "A week There one Night"! Scotty Vi D.J. Ju

AS HEARD ON ...

WHBQ

M.C. DEWEY PHILLIPS

EXTRA ORDINARY MPHS D.J.

EARLY CAREER

1954 (cont.)

Along with Scotty and Bill, Elvis records at Sun Studios. The songs don't work until Elvis sings Arthur "Big Boy" Crudup's "That's All Right." Sam Phillips immediately spots a winner and gets them to work on the song before recording it.

July 8: Disc jockey Dewey Philips—no relation of Sam—plays "That's All Right" on his show on WHBQ radio. The response is electrifying and Elvis is driven to the studio where Dewey interviews him on air. The remarkable thing about the song is that most people think that the singer must be black—it's only when Dewey identifies Elvis as an ex-Humes High School student that people realize he's white. At a time of segregation, this leads to difficulties when the single is released.

July 12: Elvis signs a contract naming Scotty Moore as his first manager.

July 19: The single "That's All Right" and "Blue Moon of Kentucky" (suggested as the B-side by Bill Black)—are issued. It reaches the top 10 on local charts in Nashville and Memphis and as far afield as New Orleans.

July 30: Elvis' first billing lights up the night sky when the threesome (Elvis, Scotty, and Bill) opens third at a Slim Whitman show. They will gig throughout the summer, regularly at the Eagle's Nest in Memphis. Elvis' trademark stage performance is a scandalous sensation and he grows in confidence. All the while, Sam Phillips is on the road selling the single.

August 7: Billboard reviews the single and talks of Elvis as "a strong new talent."

August 19: Back at Sun Studios, the three performers record three more songs.

September 11–12: And today, they record another seven, including both tracks on the second single.

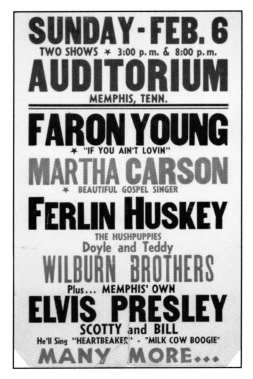

Concert poster for the **Louisiana Hayride** *on March 19, 1955*

September 25: "Good Rockin' Tonight" and "I Don't Care If the Sun Don't Shine" are released.

October 2: Elvis appears at the Grand Ole Opry, but to his disappointment the crowd doesn't go wild.

October 16: But the story is very different when he appears on the *Grand Ole Opry*'s rival, the *Louisiana Hayride*. The crowd reacts enthusiastically. The *Hayride* was broadcast live on Saturdays over KWKH Radio from Shreveport, Louisiana, and was carried by nearly 200 other radio stations over half the United States. Elvis' success is immediate. House drummer, D.J. Fontana, complements the threesome.

November 6: Because of his continued success on the *Hayride*, Elvis signs a contract for 52 Saturday shows. The trio becomes full-time musicians. Elvis buys a 1942 Martin D18 acoustic guitar from O.K. Houck Piano Co., who gives him part as an exchange on the Martin 000-18 he'd bought there in the summer when he traded in his first guitar. The *Hayride* contract had a practical downside in that it restricted the group from traveling and touring any significant distance.

November 26: Elvis sends a telegram to his father, Vernon: "HI BABIES HERE'S THE MONEY TO PAY THE BILLS STOP DON'T TELL NO ONE HOW MUCH I SENT I WILL SEND MORE NEXT WEEK STOP THERE IS A CARD IN THE MAIL STOP LOVE ELVIS."

1955

January 1: Elvis signs a management contract with Bob Neal.

January 11: "Colonel" Tom Parker hears about Elvis from DJ Ernest Hackworth of Texarkana, Arkansas, whose stage name is "Uncle Dudley."

January 15: Parker meets Elvis, having traveled to Shreveport to watch him in concert.

January 29: "Milkcow Blues Boogie" and "You're A Heartbreaker" are released.

Elvis Presley and Colonel Tom Parker in 1955

Elvis in Las Vegas, April 1956

EARLY CAREER

1955 (cont.)

March 23: Elvis auditions for *Arthur Godfrey's Talent Scouts* show in New York. He is rejected—as was Buddy Holly in 1957.

May 6: Elvis takes girlfriend Dixie Locke to her high-school prom.

May 14: "Baby Let's Play House" and "I'm Left, You're Right, She's Gone" are released. The single will reach #5 on Billboard's U.S. Country chart and will later inspire Led Zeppelin's Jimmy Page to take up the guitar.

June: Elvis replaces his Martin D-18 guitar with a D-28. He'll use the D-28 until at least November 1956.

June 17: Bob Neal agrees that Parker will exclusively handle Elvis' bookings and that they'll try to sign him with a major record label. Neal doesn't realize he now has a tiger by the tail.

July 7: Elvis takes possession of a pink Cadillac Fleetwood Sixty to replace his car that burnt out in early June.

July 22: RCA offers $12,000 for Elvis' contract.

July 26: Elvis meets June Juanico at a concert in Biloxi. He'll date her into 1956.

July 31: William V. "Red" Robertson takes photographs during a concert at Fort Homer Hesterly Armory in Tampa, Florida. One of the photos—the famous "tonsil" shot—will end up on his debut album cover.

August 1: Elvis plays Tupelo, Mississippi, for the first time since his youthful performance at the age of 10.

August 8: Drummer D.J. Fontana joins the band full time.

August 15: Elvis signs a new management contract with Bob Neal that makes Parker his special advisor.

Elvis Presley, Bill Black, Scotty Moore, and Sam Phillip, February 3, 1955

Dewey Phillips and Elvis Presley at Ellis Auditorium in Memphis, February 6, 1955

Elvis in Las Vegas, April 1956

EARLY CAREER

1955 (cont.)

August 20: "I Forgot to Remember to Forget" and "Mystery Train" are released. The A-side of this single will be Elvis' first #1 hit on Billboard's Country chart. "Mystery Train" will reach #11. The single will spend 39 weeks on the charts.

September 15: Neal signs Elvis up for another one-year contract with the *Hayride* at the improved rate of $200 a show.

September 17: But after an argument with Parker, Neal relinquishes his contractual arrangement with Elvis, thus ensuring Parker's complete control. Neal will remain involved with Elvis until early in 1956.

September 24: Elvis gets his first top billing—at the *Louisiana Hayride*.

October 16: Elvis plays in support of Bill Haley, whose "Rock Around the Clock" tops the charts.

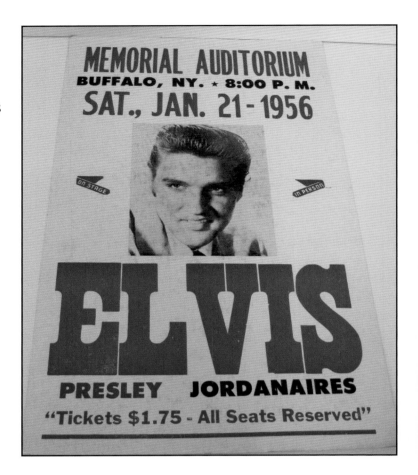

Elvis Presley in 1956

October 24: Parker contacts Sam Phillips to agree to a price for Elvis' contract.

October 29: They agree on a price of $35,000.

November 10: Elvis attends the 4th annual Country Music Disk Jockey Convention in Nashville where he is voted the year's most promising male artist. Songwriter Mae Boren Axton visits Elvis in his hotel room and plays him a demo of a song called "Heartbreak Hotel."

November 14: Parker talks Elvis and films with the William Morris Agency.

November 21: At Sun Studios—with his parents because he is still, at 20 years old, a minor—Elvis signs with RCA Records who will almost immediately (in December) re-release the five Sun singles. Elvis gets a bonus of $5,000 on top of the contract price. At the same time, Elvis signs with Hill and Range Publishing Company to set up Elvis Presley Music, Inc., which will receive a portion of the songwriters' royalties if Elvis records their songs.

1956

January 10: Elvis' first recording session for RCA in Nashville lays down "I Got a Woman," "Heartbreak Hotel," and "Money Honey." The band is beefed up by the inclusion of a pianist (Floyd Cramer), Chet Atkins on guitar, and three backing singers.

January 21: Record Mirror prints the first picture of Elvis to be published in the U.K.

January 27: The single "Heartbreak Hotel" and "I Was the One" is released by RCA. The response is huge and immediate. The new single sells over 300,000 copies in its first three weeks, going to #1 on Billboard's pop singles and country charts and #5 on the R&B chart. It will be the best-selling single of 1956, selling over 1 million copies. It will pay for a new home for Elvis' parents, and today it has been certified double platinum. It also reaches #1 in Canada and Italy.

Love Me Tender

The only film in which Elvis did not get top billing. Also the only film he made where his character was killed on screen.

Director	Robert D. Webb Stanley Hough (assistant)
Producer	David Weisbart
Screenplay by	Robert Buckner
Story by	Maurice Geraghty
Starring	Richard Egan Debra Paget Elvis Presley
Music by	Lionel Newman
Cinematography	Leo Tover
Editing by	Hugh S. Fowler
Distributed by	20th Century Fox
Release date	November 15, 1956

Elvis Presley in 1956

1956 (cont.)

January 28: Elvis makes his first network TV appearance on CBS TV's *Stage Show*, recorded in New York City. He receives $1,250 for the first of six shows set up by Parker between now and March 24.

February 23: Elvis collapses from exhaustion after performing at The Baseball Park in Jacksonville, Florida.

March 15: Elvis and Colonel Parker sign a new contract that gives Parker 25% of Elvis' earnings.

March 20: The Presley family moves into 1034 Audubon Drive in Memphis.

March 23: The album *Elvis Presley* is released. Side 1 is "Blue Suede Shoes," "I'm Counting on You," "I Got A Woman," "One-Sided Love Affair," "I Love You Because," and "Just Because." Side 2 is "Tutti Frutti," "Tryin' to Get to You," "I'm Gonna Sit Right Down and Cry (Over You)," "I'll Never Let You Go (Little Darlin')," "Blue Moon," and "Money Honey." Elvis' first album spends 10 weeks at #1 on Billboard's album charts—the first rock 'n' roll album to do so—selling a million copies. It is certified gold in 1966 and platinum in 2011. The same day RCA issues two EPs with the same tracks as the LP; RCA would do this for all of Elvis' albums until 1960. Between 1961 and 1967, only six EPs were released—all movie soundtrack recordings. [For space reasons, these EPs haven't been identified in this timeline.]

March 24: Presley visits his friend Carl Perkins in the hospital in Dover, Delaware, after a car crash.

March 25: Elvis flies to Hollywood and screen tests for Paramount Studios from March 26 to 28.

March 31: Elvis' makes his last regular appearance on the *Louisiana Hayride*, the show that served so well to foster his talent and make him a star. The band was constantly gigging so that returning each Saturday night to Shreveport became impossible.

Loving You

A delivery man is discovered by a music publicist and country-western musician who wants to promote the talented newcomer to fame and fortune. *Loving You* is Elvis' second movie, his first in Technicolor, and his first with top billing.

Director	Hal Kanter
Producer	Hal B. Wallis
Screenplay by	Herbert Baker, Hal Kanter
Story by	Mary Agnes Thompson
Starring	Elvis Presley, Lizabeth Scott, Wendell Corey
Music by	Walter Scharf
Cinematography	Charles Lang
Editing by	Howard A. Smith
Studio	Hal Wallis Productions
Distributed by	Paramount Pictures
Release date	July 9, 1957

Elvis Presley in 1956

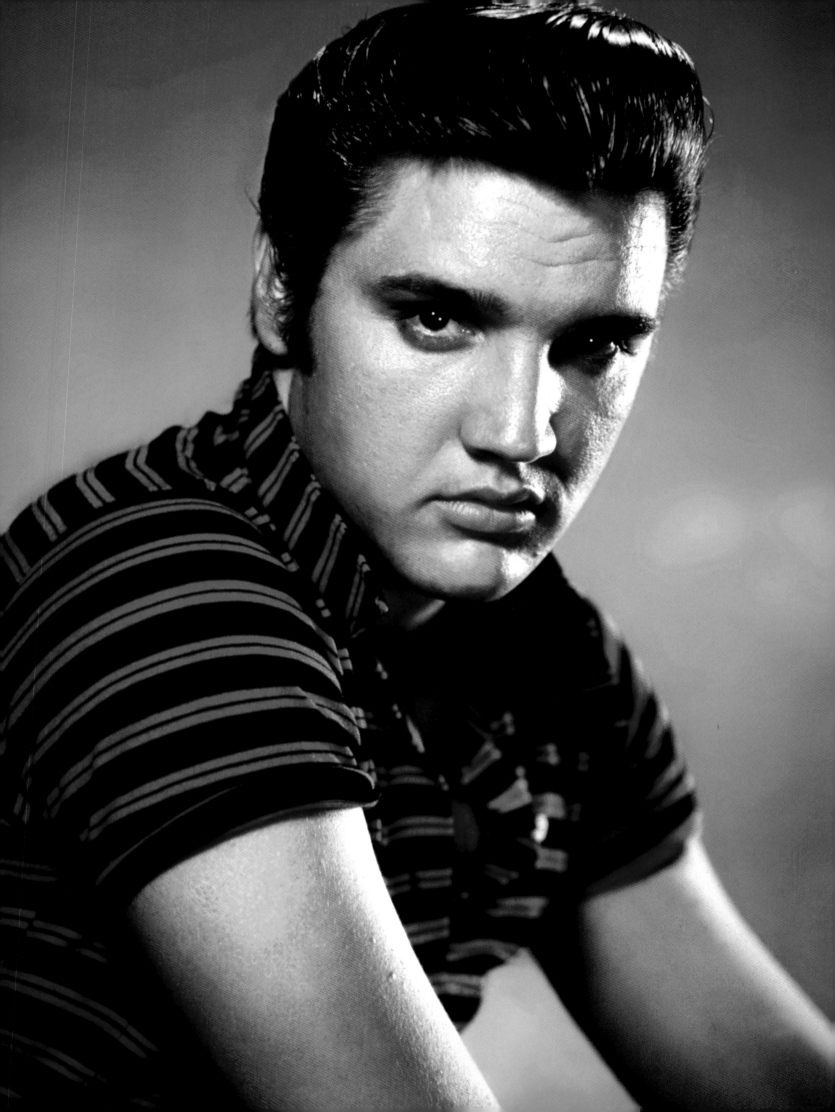

1956 (cont.)

April 3: Elvis sings "Heartbreak Hotel" and "Blue Suede Shoes" on NBC's *The Milton Berle Show* from the aircraft carrier USS Hancock.

April 15–21: Gigging in Texas, Elvis and his band play San Antonio on the 15th, Corpus Christi on the 16th, Waco on the 17th; then Tulsa, Oklahoma, on the 18th and Oklahoma City on the 19th; then back to Texas, stopping in Fort Worth on the 20th, and playing two shows in Houston on the 21st.

April 23–May 6: Elvis spends two weeks at the New Frontier Hotel in Las Vegas. During the stint, the single "Heartbreak Hotel" and the album *Elvis Presley*, go to #1 on the Billboard single and album pop charts, respectively. Elvis doesn't rock Las Vegas, whose audience is older than his usual fans.

April 25: Elvis signs a movie contract with Hal Wallis and Paramount Pictures. It's for one movie with options on six more. The payments, starting at $15,000, get bigger for each movie, with the seventh due to be worth $100,000. In fact Parker managed to get bonus payments from the studio. Parker also has the right to contract one film a year outside Paramount.

May: "Heartbreak Hotel" is Elvis' first U.K. hit that reaches #2. Later in the month "Blue Suede Shoes" reaches the top 10.

May 12: "My Baby Left Me" and "I Want You, I Need You, I Love You" are released and become Elvis' second #1 single (on the Country charts), reaching #3 on the Billboard Top 100.

June 5: A second appearance on *The Milton Berle Show* includes a version of "Hound Dog" that leads to a storm of protest by the critics and leads to the "Elvis the Pelvis" epithet.

July 1: Elvis appears on NBC's *The Steve Allen Show* and sings "Hound Dog" to a Bassett hound while dressed in a tuxedo. Later he will describe his performance as ridiculous.

Elvis Presley in 1956

Elvis performing in Dayton, Ohio, 1956

Elvis Presley in 1956

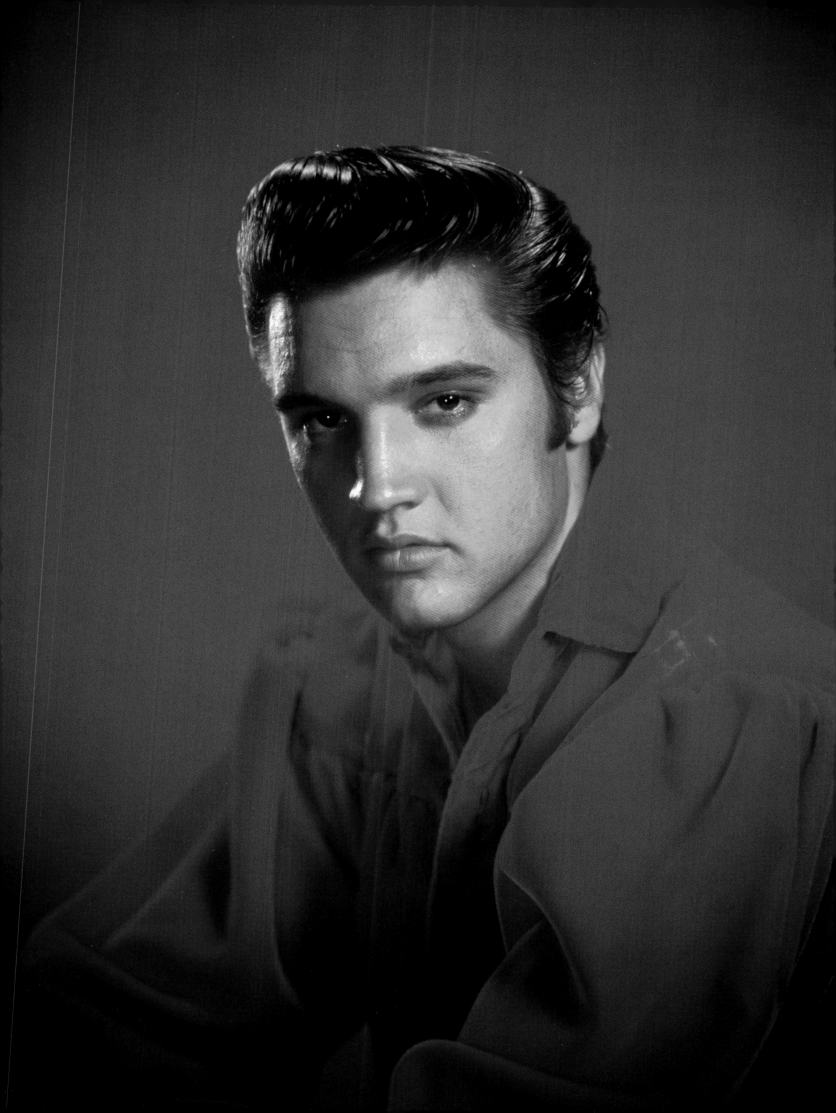

Elvis Presley performing in Dayton, Ohio, 1956

Elvis Presley in 1956

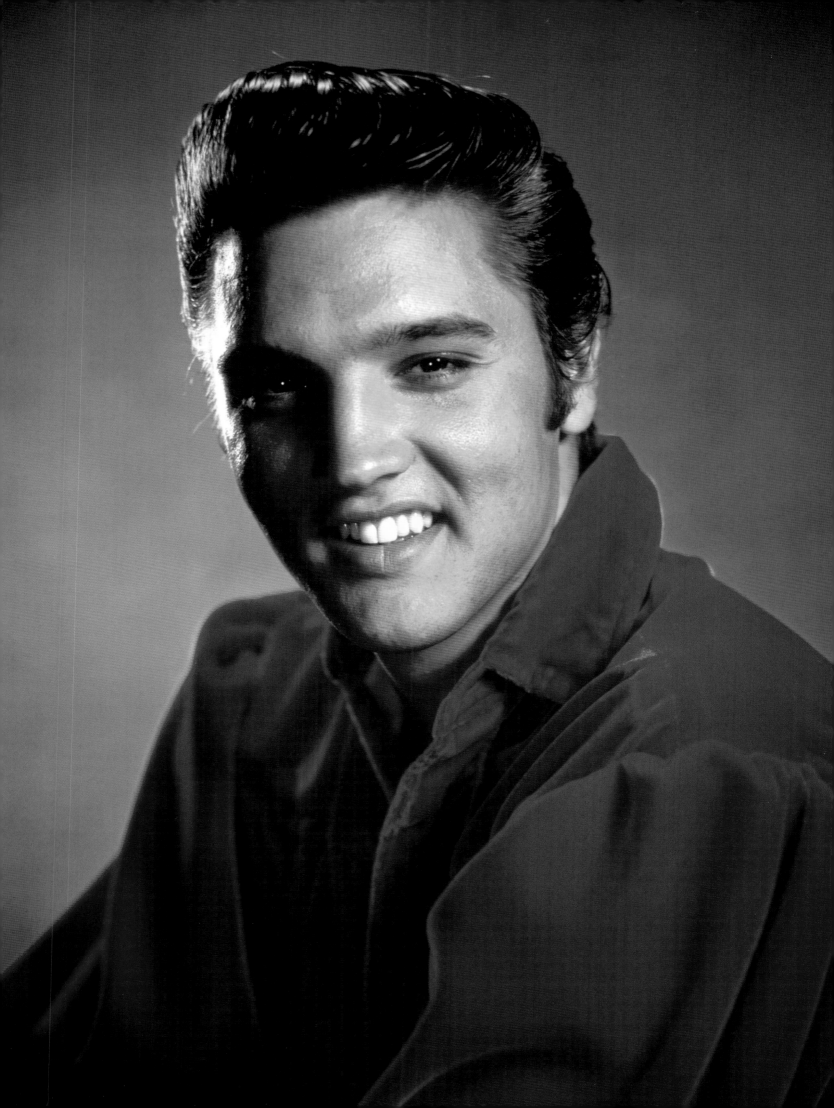

Elvis, taking oath in court following an altercation, with Ed Hopper and Aubrey Brown (on left), 1956

Elvis shopping for clothes in 1956

Elvis Presley in 1956

Elvis Presley and Natalie Wood in 1956

1956 (cont.)

July 21: "Hound Dog" and "Don't Be Cruel" are released—the obvious next single after the furor. Backing him on the record are the Jordanaires, a gospel quartet who will work regularly with him in the studio and on tour for the next decade. His classic "Hound Dog" is rated 19th on Rolling Stone's list of The 500 Greatest Songs of All Time. Both sides of the single go to #1 (for 11 weeks) and sell multi-platinum millions. The single also reaches #1 in Canada and Italy.

July/August: Ed Sullivan—who had expressed his dislike of Elvis' music and stage act—is forced to backtrack after seeing Elvis' success on his rivals' shows. Parker and he thrash out a three-show deal for the then remarkable sum of $50,000.

August: Because they can't find a vehicle, Paramount allows Parker to negotiate a deal with 20th Century Fox for Elvis' first film with options on two more. Elvis receives $100,000 for the first film, *Love Me Tender*. The second film, *Flaming Star*, will net him $200,000, and the third, *Wild in the Country*, will earn him $250,000.

August 10–11: Because of the public outcry, Judge Marion Gooding watches Elvis' first show in Jacksonville, Florida, and suggests that he tones down his act. At the second show, Elvis just wiggles his little finger—the crowd reacts as wildly as before.

August 22: Elvis begins his first film, *Love Me Tender*, a Civil War drama that is retitled from the original *The Reno Brothers* in order to make the most of Elvis' newest single. Elvis is billed third, but his role, originally offered to Robert Wagner and Jeffrey Hunter, is beefed up to match his new popularity.

September 8: "Blue Suede Shoes" and "Tutti Frutti" are released. These songs were a hit for his friend Carl Perkins so Elvis requests that his versions are held back in order not to detract from Perkins' success. Elvis' version reaches #20 and is certified gold in 1999. The single is also another #1 hit in Italy.

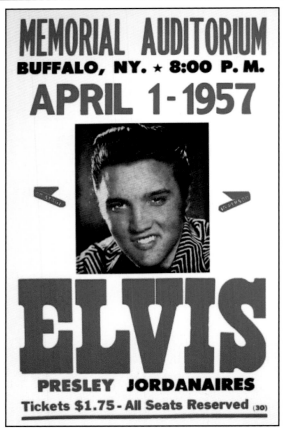

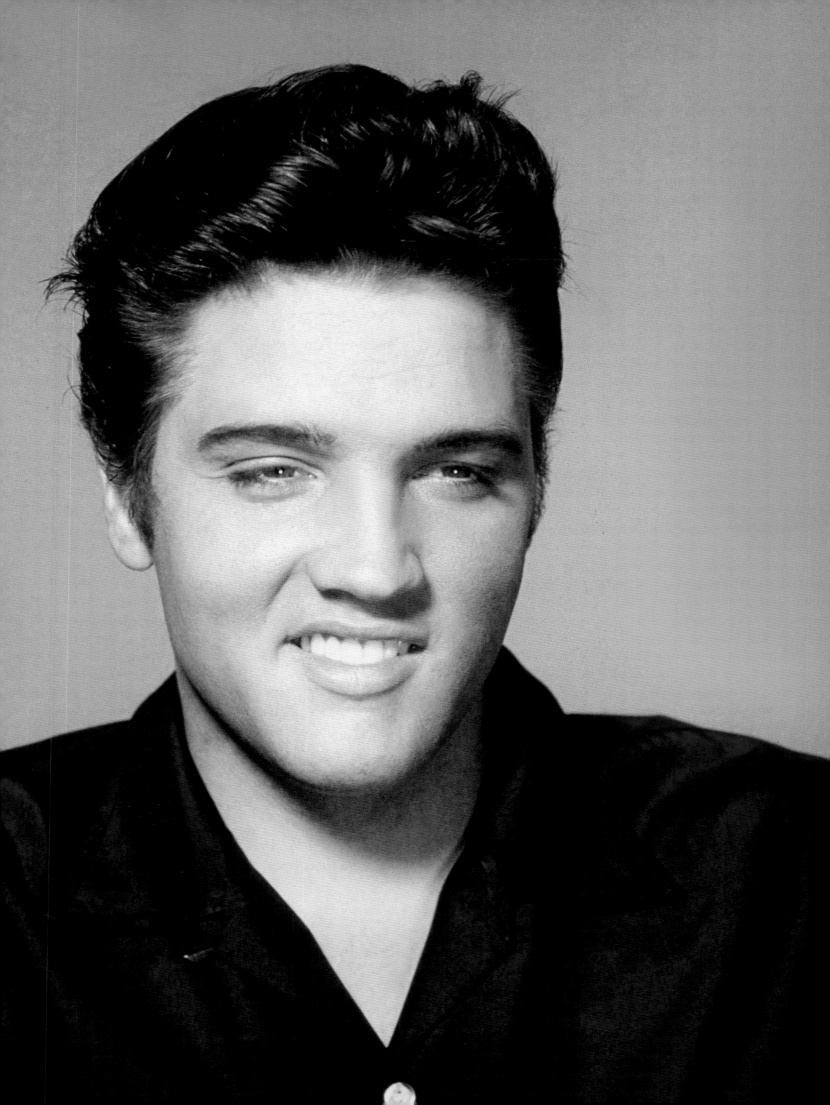

EARLY CAREER

1956 (cont.)

September 9: The first of his three appearances on *The Ed Sullivan Show* takes place without Ed Sullivan (actor Charles Laughton takes over), who has had a car crash. The show is a massive success, attracting some 60 million viewers—80% of the national viewing audience. His performance of "Love Me Tender" ensures huge advance orders for the single (over a million).

September 21: "Hound Dog" becomes Elvis' third top 10 single in the U.K., reaching #2.

September 26: Elvis' origins are remembered at Elvis Presley Day in Tupelo, Mississippi. Elvis performs at the Mississippi-Alabama Fair and Dairy Show, just as he did at age 10, but to a much larger audience controlled by over a hundred National Guardsmen.

October: His guitarist, Scotty, is endorsed by Gibson guitars, and Elvis changes his guitar to a Gibson J-200. Scotty picked it up for him from O.K. Houck's Piano Co. in Memphis. Elvis will use this guitar for many years. It will be refurbished in 1960 when he leaves the U.S. Army, and he will use it on his NBC TV Special.

October 6: "Love Me Tender" and "Any Way You Want Me (That's How I Will Be)" are released to huge orders assuring immediate gold certification and a #1 spot for five weeks in the U.S.; the single also reaches #1 in Canada.

October 18: Elvis spends time in jail after a fracas at a service station in Memphis. He is cleared in court and his assailants are fined.

October 19: His second album, *Elvis*, is released. Side 1 is "Rip It Up," "Love Me," "When My Blue Moon Turns to Gold Again," "Long Tall Sally," "First in Line," and "Paralyzed." Side 2 is "So Glad You're Mine," "Old Shep," "Ready Teddy," "Anyplace Is Paradise," "How's the World Treating You?" and "How Do You Think I Feel?" The album reaches #1 on the Billboard Top Pop Albums chart and spends five weeks there. Certified gold in 1960, it reaches platinum in 2011.

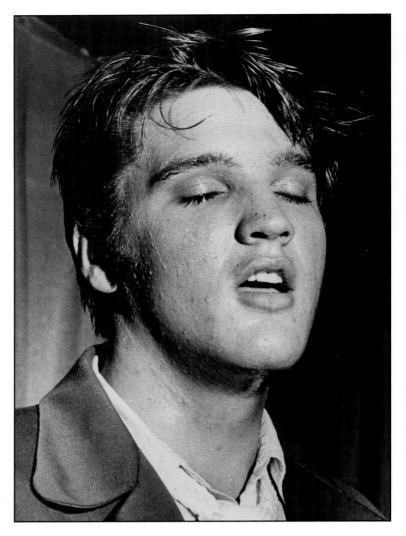

Elvis shows his new $100,000 home, Graceland, to the Hollywood starlet Yvonne Lime, who flew in to spend Easter weekend with Presley and his parents, in Memphis, April 19, 1957.

Elvis Presley in 1957

Jailhouse Rock

A young man, played by Elvis, is sentenced to prison for manslaughter and while there is mentored in music by his prison cellmate. After his release from jail he looks for a job as a club singer and meets a musical promoter who launches his career. But as he develops his musical abilities and becomes a star, his self-centered personality begins to affect his relationships.

Director	Richard Thorpe
Producer	Pandro S. Berman
Screenplay by	Guy Trosper
Story by	Nedrick Young
Starring	Elvis Presley, Judy Tyler, Mickey Shaughnessy
Music by	Jeff Alexander
Cinematography	Robert J. Bronner
Editing by	Ralph E. Winters
Studio	Avon Productions
Distributed by	Metro-Goldwyn-Mayer
Release date	October 17, 1957 (USA)

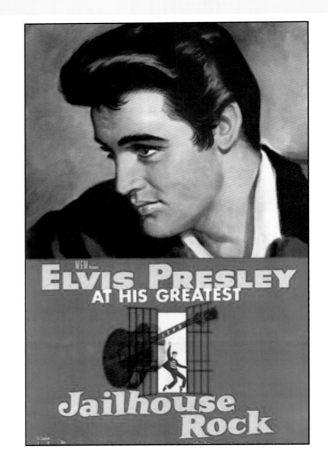

Elvis in Jailhouse Rock, *1957*

The songwriters Mike Stoller and Jerry Leiber with Elvis

Jailhouse Rock, *1957*

Elvis and Judy Tyler in Jailhouse Rock *directed by Richard Thorpe* [Metro-Goldwyn-Meyer], 1957

Elvis and Judy Tyler in Jailhouse Rock, *1957*

Elvis Presley in 1957

Four photos of Elvis and Sophia Loren in 1958

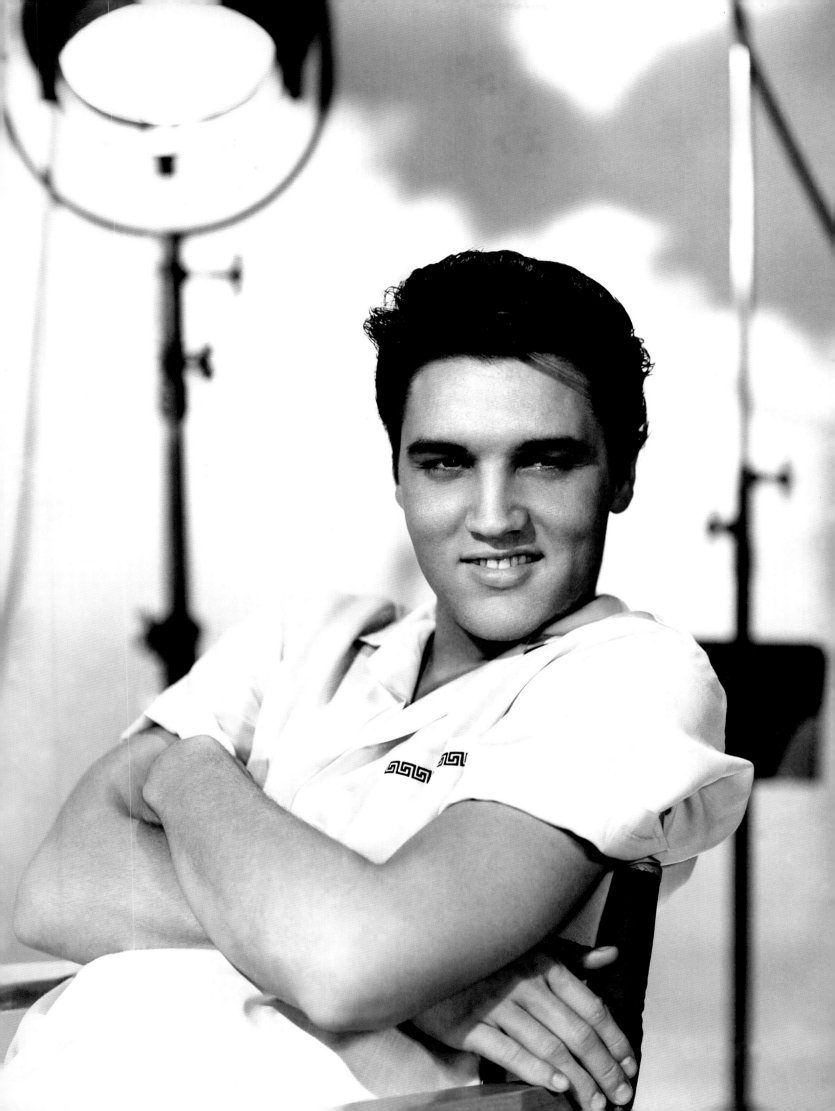

MILITARY SERVICE

Elvis flanked by his parents, Gladys and Vernon Presley on March 24, 1958, around the beginning of his military service.

Just like every other military inductee, Elvis undergoes an eye exam.

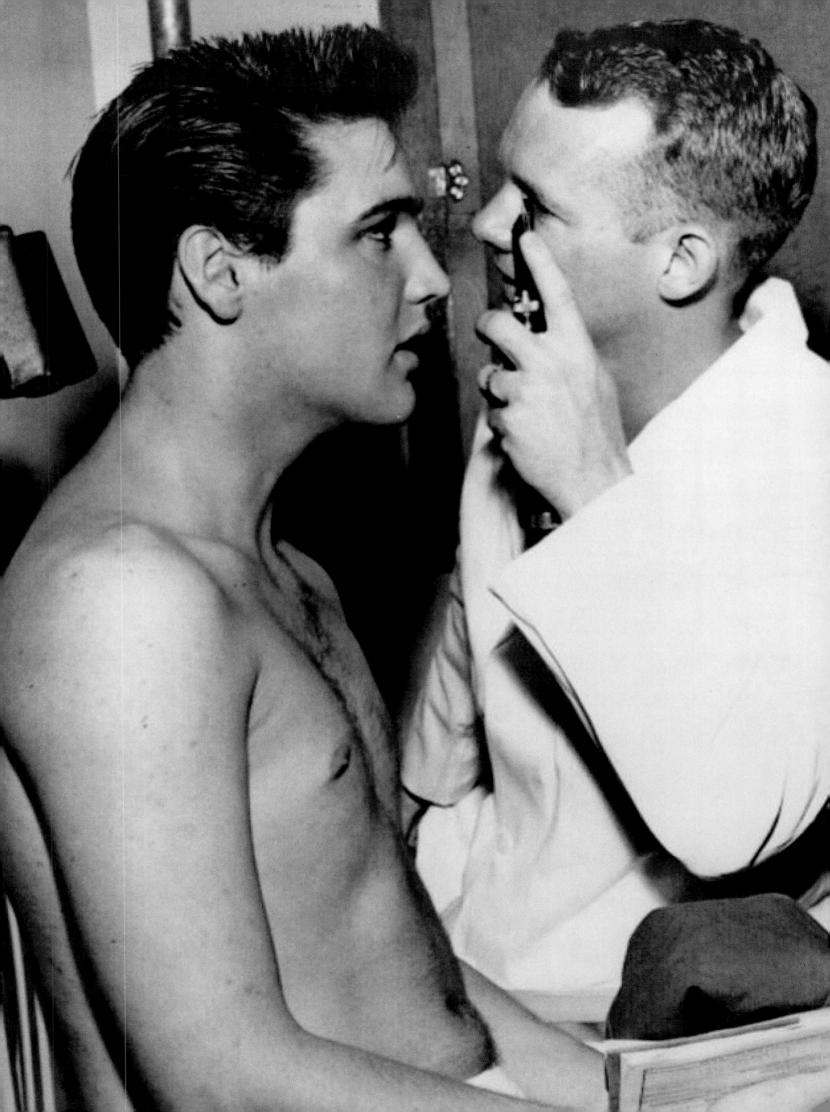

Elvis is sworn in to the U.S. Army at Fort Chaffee, Arkansas, in March 1958. He served for two years until March 1960.

Elvis did his country proud by admirably serving in the U.S. Army.

MILITARY SERVICE

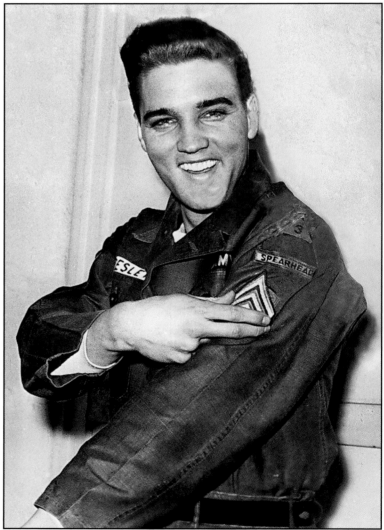

Elvis tries his helmet on for size—and his new sargent's stripes—(above) and reads a letter from a fan (right).

Elvis getting into a BMW 507 sports car, December 21, 1958

Elvis with his future wife, Priscilla, then only 16 years old (top facing page)

Elvis in uniform in Friedberg, Germany, 1958

Sargent Presley at a news conference

*Frank Sinatra welcomes Elvis home
from military service on his TV show.*

THE KING IS CROWNED

Elvis Presley with comic Lou Costello and Jane Russell

Dean Martin, Shirley MacLaine, and Elvis

October 28: Elvis appears for a second time on *The Ed Sullivan Show*.

November 15: *Love Me Tender*, his first movie, premiers at the Paramount Theater in New York City. Panned by critics, it is nevertheless a huge box office success.

December 4: The famous "Million Dollar Quartet" session at Sun Records gets Carl Perkins, Jerry Lee Lewis, and Elvis jamming. Johnny Cash is also there for the photo.

December 13: *Love Me Tender* premiers in London.

December 16: Elvis returns to Shreveport for a final *Louisiana Hayride* performance. At the end of the show, announcer Horace Logan tries to get fans back to their seats by telling them, "Elvis has left the building."

December 31: *The Wall Street Journal* reports sales of Elvis merchandise have grossed $22 million.

1957

January 4: Elvis has his pre-induction Army draft physical at Kenney Veterans Hospital in Memphis.

January 6: His third appearance on *The Ed Sullivan Show* is the last live television performance Elvis will ever do. Ed Sullivan, his one-time critic, is enthusiastic in his praise for Elvis, a strong endorsement in the entertainment industry.

January 8: The draft board announces that Elvis is classified 1A and will be drafted in 1957.

January 12: "Too Much" and "Playing for Keeps" are released. The single peaks at #1 on the Hot 100 chart.

January 14: Jerry Leiber and Mike Stoller (who wrote "Hound Dog" and "Love Me") are commissioned to write songs for Elvis' next movie, *Loving You*, which he starts filming on the 21st.

King Creole

This film is about a 19-year-old who gets mixed up with crooks and is involved with two women. Elvis later indicated that the role of Danny Fisher in *King Creole* was his favorite.

Director	Michael Curtiz
Producer	Hal B. Wallis
Screenplay by	Herbert Baker Michael V. Gazzo
Based on	*A Stone for Danny Fisher* by Harold Robbins
Starring	Elvis Presley, Carolyn Jones, Walter Matthau
Music by	Walter Scharf
Cinematography	Russell Harlan
Editing by	Warren Low
Studio	Hal Wallis Productions
Distributed by	Paramount Pictures
Release date	July 2, 1958 (USA)

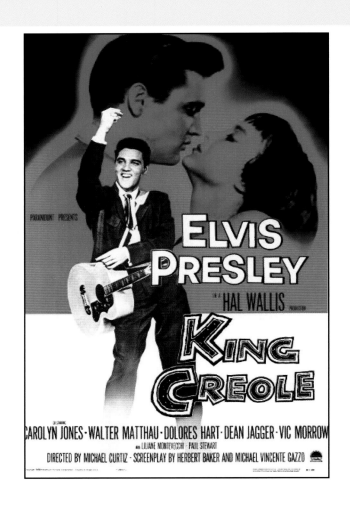

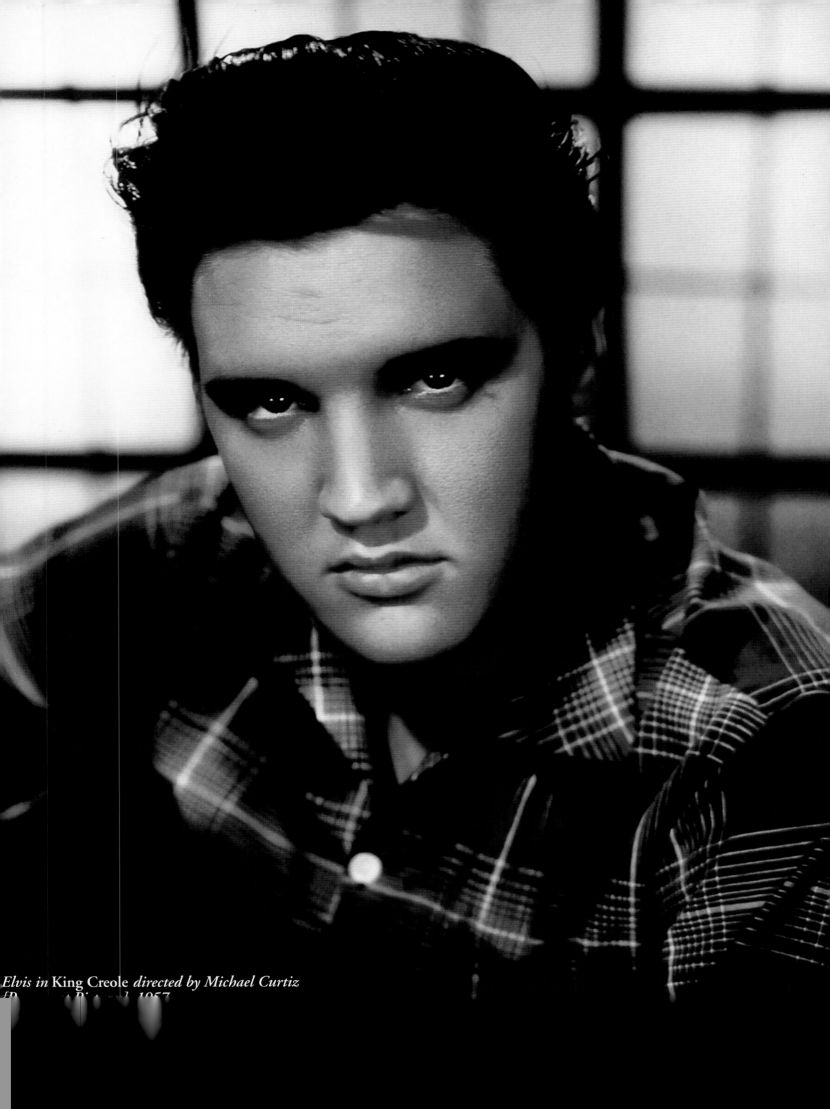

Elvis in King Creole *directed by Michael Curtiz*
(Paramount Pictures), 1957

1957 (cont.)

February: Parker negotiates a deal with MGM for *Jailhouse Rock*. Elvis gets $250,000 and 50% of the film's profits.

March 17: Needing to find a more private place for the family because Audubon Drive is swamped by fans, Elvis' parents talk to a real estate agent, Virginia Grant, who shows them Graceland.

March 19: Elvis' parents like Graceland so they visit again with Elvis. They sign the sales agreement on the spot.

March 23: "All Shook Up" and "That's When Your Heartaches Begin" are released and the single goes to #1 on the pop chart for eight weeks and tops the R&B chart for four weeks. It is certified double platinum and is also Elvis' fourth #1 hit in both Canada and Italy.

April 2: Elvis appears outside the U.S. for the first time, performing two shows at Canada Maple Leaf Gardens in Toronto and two more shows in Ottawa the next day.

April 22: Graceland's "Music Gates" (designed by Abe Saucer and made by Memphis Doors, Inc.) are delivered and fitted.

April 30: Work on MGM's *Jailhouse Rock* soundtrack starts.

May 16: Graceland is ready for habitation. Vernon and Gladys move in, but Elvis' move is delayed because of work commitments.

June: "All Shook Up" becomes Elvis' first U.K. #1 hit.

June 10: "Teddy Bear" and "Loving You" are released. Another multi-platinum seller, Elvis' third #1 hit of 1957 sits atop the charts for seven weeks and goes to #1 on the R&B and Country charts as well. In the U.K., it reaches #3, and in Canada, #1.

June 26: Elvis finally spends his first night in Graceland.

G.I. Blues

Mainly filmed at the Paramount Pictures studio, the movie did include some pre-production scenery shot on location in Germany before Elvis' release from the army. The movie reached #2 on the *Variety* weekly national box office chart in 1960. It also won a 2nd place Laurel Award in the category of Top Musical of 1960.

Director	Norman Taurog
Producer	Hal B. Wallis
Written by	Edmund Beloin Henry Garson
Starring	Elvis Presley Juliet Prowse Robert Ivers
Music by	Joseph J. Lilley
Cinematography	Loyal Griggs
Editing by	Warren Low
Studio	Hal Wallis Productions
Distributed by	Paramount Pictures
Release date	August 18, 1960 (USA)

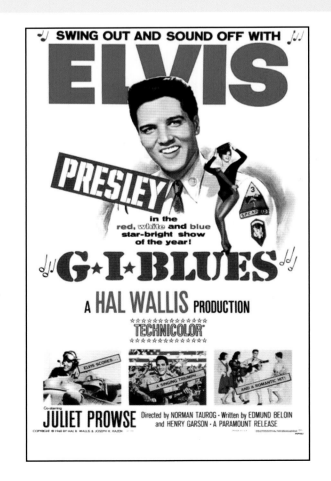

THE KING IS CROWNED

July 1: Elvis' third album, *Loving You*, is released. Side 1 is "Mean Woman Blues," "Teddy Bear," "Loving You," "Got a Lot O' Livin' to Do," "Lonesome Cowboy," "Hot Dog," and "Party." Side 2 is "Blueberry Hill," "True Love," "Don't Leave Me Now," "Have I Told You Lately That I Love You?" and "I Need You So." The album spends 10 weeks at #1 on the Billboard Top Pop Albums chart and was certified gold in 1968, helped of course by the movie of the same name.

July 9: *Loving You*, Elvis' second movie, premieres in Memphis and opens nationwide on July 30.

August 27: Elvis calls Anita Wood (nicknamed "Little") "number one with me" as he says goodbye before boarding a train for his West Coast tour. Anita will date Elvis until after his de-mobilization from the U.S. Army.

August 31: The second gig of his West Coast tour is in Vancouver, Canada. Surprisingly, this is the last time Elvis will ever perform outside the U.S. Many theories exist as to why he will not play abroad, especially after being offered $1 million for doing so in Australia in 1974. It certainly wasn't a fear of flying. One theory is that Colonel Parker was worried about getting a passport because he was an illegal immigrant.

September 7: Money matters with Scotty Moore and Billy Black come to a head at the end of the tour and the two Blue Moon Boys resign by sending Elvis registered letters.

September 13: The story is reported in the *Memphis Press-Scimitar* alongside a photograph of Anita Wood sporting the huge sapphire and diamond ring Elvis gave her.

September 14: Elvis goes to the press with an open message in which he says, "Scotty, I hope you fellows have good luck. I will give you fellows good recommendations. If you had come to me, we would have worked things out. I would have always taken care of you. But you went to the papers and tried to make me look bad instead of coming to me so we could work things out. All I can say to you is 'good luck.'" He starts auditioning new musicians and is linked up with Hank Garland from Nashville.

September 23: "Jailhouse Rock" and "Treat Me Nice" are released. Leiber and Stoller score another huge hit for Elvis with these songs. The single reaches #1 on both sides of the Atlantic—for seven weeks in the U.S. and three in the U.K, but not until 1958. The single is the first to enter the U.K. charts in first place. It also reaches #1 in Canada and South Africa.

September 27: Elvis plays at the Fairground in Tupelo—a benefit for the proposed Elvis Presley Youth Recreation Center—with Garland on guitar, D.J. on drums, and D.J.'s friend Chuck Wiggington on bass. He decides to make amends with Scotty and Billy and by the end of the month they are back together.

October 15: Elvis' *Christmas Album* is released. Side 1 includes "Santa Claus Is Back in Town," "White Christmas," "Here Comes Santa Claus," "I'll Be Home for Christmas," "Blue Christmas," and "Santa, Bring My Baby Back." Side 2 includes "O Little Town of Bethlehem," "Silent Night," "Peace in the Valley," "I Believe," "Take My Hand, Precious Lord," and "It Is No Secret." Elvis' fourth album spends four weeks at #1 in the U.S. and to date has sold over 13 million copies in the U.S. It was the first Elvis title to be certified diamond.

October 17: MGM's *Jailhouse Rock*, Elvis' third movie, opens in Memphis, opening nationally on November 8. Its position at the ox office—#14 for the year—is helped by the success of its single.

November 10–11: Elvis performs in Hawaii, his last public appearance before entering the Army.

December 20: Elvis receives his draft notice, but is granted a 60-day deferment on the 27th to finish *King Creole*.

December 30: "Don't" and "I Beg of You" are released. This single becomes Elvis' 10th #1 hit in the U.S. and also reached #1 in Canada and South Africa.

1958

January–early March: Elvis is filming the movie *King Creole*. He's in good company with his famous co-stars: Walter Matthau, Carolyn Jones, Vic Morrow, Jan Shepard, Paul Stewart, Dolores Hart, and Dean Jagger.

THE KING IS CROWNED

February 1: The last time Elvis plays with bassist Bill Black. Black dies in 1965.

March 24: Elvis inducted into the U.S. Army at the Memphis Draft Board. His serial number is 53310761. The press is out in force.

March 25: The most famous haircut in the world? Probably. It takes place at Fort Chaffee, Arkansas. Elvis is assigned to 2nd Medium Tank Battalion, 2nd Armored Division, which is nicknamed "Hell on Wheels."

March 28: Elvis goes to Fort Hood, Texas, for basic training. He asks to be treated like any other soldier—but his family follows him, living in an off-base trailer.

April 7: "Wear My Ring Around Your Neck" and "Doncha' Think It's Time" are released. The single just fails to reach #1, peaking at #2 in the Hot 100, although it does make it to #1 in the R&B charts.

May 31–June 13: Elvis has his first furlough and spends some of the time in the Nashville recording studio—his last recording session until 1960. One of the songs recorded is "A Big Hunk O' Love."

June 14: His mother, Gladys, is diagnosed with hepatitis and hospitalized. Elvis returns to Fort Hood for advanced tank training. The family moves to Killeen, Texas, on the 26th and Elvis lives with them off base.

June 16: "Hard-Headed Woman" and "Don't Ask Me Why" are released. The single reaches #1 on the Hot 100, #2 in the U.K. and in Australia, and #1 in Canada.

July 2: The movie *King Creole* opens nationally to good reviews.

August 8: Gladys returns to Memphis with acute hepatitis. Elvis is given compassionate leave on August 12 to be with her. She dies on August 14 and is buried the next day at Forest Hill Cemetery, near Graceland. Elvis is devastated.

August 24: Elvis returns to Fort Hood.

October: Parker renegotiates the Paramount contract. Elvis' salary is raised to $175,000 for *GI Blues* and he will get a royalty.

September 11: Elvis is posted to the 1st Medium Tank Battalion, 32nd Armor, 3rd Armored Division in West Germany.

September 19: He leaves Fort Worth by train for Germany on the day his *King Creole* album is released. Side 1 includes "King Creole," "As Long as I Have You," "Hard-Headed Woman," "Trouble," and "Dixieland Rock." Side 2 includes "Don't Ask Me Why," "Lover Doll," "Crawfish," "Young Dreams," "Steadfast, Loyal, and True," and "New Orleans." *King Creole* reaches #2 on the album charts.

October 1: Troopship USS General George M. Randall arrives in Bremerhaven and Elvis is in Germany. He will be stationed in Friedberg for 18 months, living off base in Hotel Grünewald in Bad Nauheim with his father, grandmother Minnie Mae, and some friends from Memphis.

October 23: Elvis watches a Bill Haley gig and goes backstage. He attends again on the 29th.

October 27: "I Got Stung" and "One Night" are released. This single will reach #4 on the Billboard singles chart and #1 in Canada.

1959

Early January: Eighteen-year-old bilingual Elisabeth Stefaniak becomes Elvis' secretary and moves into Hotel Grünewald.

January 8: On his 24th birthday, Elvis is interviewed by Dick Clark on ABC's *American Bandstand*.

January: The single "One Night" and "I Got Stung" reaches #1 in the U.K.

February 3: Elvis and his extended family move into a big house in Bad Nauheim.

March 10: "A Fool Such as I" and "I Need Your Love Tonight" goes to #2 in the U.S., #1 in the U.K., Canada, Australia and South Africa.

Elvis at the Moulin Rouge in Munich, Germany, March 195

June 13–27: On a 15-day furlough, Elvis travels to Paris, meets Brigitte Bardot, visits the Moulin Rouge and the Lido Club and its Bluebell Girls. On the 20th, the club asks for its girls back in time for the show ...

July 15: ABC announces that a *Welcome Home Elvis* TV special will air in spring 1960. Elvis will be paid $125,000.

August 15: Captain Joseph Beaulieu arrives at Wiesbaden Air Force Base near Friedberg. His family includes his 14-year-old stepdaughter, Priscilla Ann.

September 13: Priscilla attends a party at Elvis' home. They meet and he immediately falls for her.

December 6: Jurgen Seydel introduces Elvis to karate. They begin bi-weekly lessons.

December 25: Priscilla gives Elvis a set of bongos as a Christmas present. Elvis gives Anita Wood a poodle.

1960

January 8: Dick Clark interviews Elvis on his birthday.

January 12–17: Elvis visits Paris again. This time he is with his karate instructor, Jurgen Seydel, while there studies with Japanese karate teacher, Tetsuji Murakami.

January 20: Elvis is promoted to sergent. He leaves on maneuvers four days later and gets his stripes on February 11.

March 2: At the end of his tour of duty, Elvis leaves by aircraft, saying goodbye to Priscilla.

March 3: Elvis sets foot on U.K. soil for the first and only time—for two hours at Prestwick Airport in Scotland. He mixes with local fans. Later that day he arrives at McGuire Air Force Base in New Jersey.

March 5: Elvis is officially discharged from active duty, leaving the army with honor having served with credit. Later, he takes a train for Memphis, arriving on March 8.

March 20: Elvis' first recording session after his discharge includes Scotty Moore and D.J. Fontana. They record the single "Stuck on You," which is rushed to the pressing plant.

March 26: Elvis receives $125,000 for a six-minute appearance in a Frank Sinatra special on ABC. Filmed today it will air on May 12.

March 28: "Stuck on You" and "Fame and Fortune" are released. The single goes to #1 on the Billboard pop charts, #2 in Norway, #3 in the U.K., and #1 in Canada, Australia, and Italy.

April 8: Elvis' 10th album, *Elvis Is Back!* is released. It reaches #2 on the Billboard albums chart and #1 in the U.K. Side 1 contains "Make Me Know It," "Fever," "The Girl of My Best Friend," "I Will Be Home Again," "Dirty, Dirty Feeling," and "Thrill of Your Love." Side 2 contains "Soldier Boy," "Such a Night," "It Feels So Right," "The Girl Next Door Went A'Walking," "Like A Baby," and "Reconsider Baby."

April 21: Elvis starts work on his fifth film, Paramount's *GI Blues*.

May 12: The Frank Sinatra Timex Special *Welcome Home, Elvis* is watched by 41.5% of the national television audience.

July 3: Vernon Presley marries Davada (Dee) Stanley, whom he met in Germany. They live at Graceland, then nearby.

July 11: "It's Now or Never" and "A Mess of Blues" are released. The single goes to #1 in the U.S. for five weeks and in the U.K. for eight weeks. The single hits #1 in Canada, Australia, Belgium, Norway, South Africa, Spain, Sweden, and Switzerland and #2 in Germany, Holland, and Italy. This is Elvis' biggest international hit to date, selling over 20 million records.

July 21: Elvis trains with, and then is awarded his first degree black belt in karate by, Hank Slomanski, a 101st Airborne Division instructor who said of Elvis' karate skills: "The kid ain't pretty, but he's tough and he's a Black Belt." Elvis will carry the certificate in his wallet until his death.

Elvis Presley in 1959

1960 (cont.)

August 1–October 7: Elvis works on his sixth movie, 20th Century Fox's *Flaming Star*, a drama with only two songs. His performance was creditable and director Don Siegel acknowledged this—but Colonel Parker wanted more music and few of his later films would stretch his acting talents.

October 1: *G.I. Blues*—Elvis' 11th album—is released. Side 1 is "Tonight Is So Right for Love," "What's She Really Like?" "Frankfort Special," "Wooden Heart," and "G.I. Blues." Side 2 is "Pocketful of Rainbows," "Shoppin' Around," "Big Boots," "Didja' Ever?" "Blue Suede Shoes," and "Doin' the Best I Can." Eventually going platinum, it went to the top of the Billboard charts at home and spent 10 weeks there. It was nominated for a Grammy.

November: Colonel Parker sets up a two-movie deal with United Artists that will pay Elvis $500,000 plus 50% of the profits for both *Follow That Dream* **and** *Kid Galahad*.

November 1: "Are You Lonesome Tonight?" and "I Gotta Know" are released. The single reaches #1 in the U.S., U.K., Canada, Australia, Belgium, and South Africa and is nominated for three Grammys.

November 3: With "It's Now or Never" Elvis becomes the first act ever to have five #1 hits in the U.K.

November 6: Elvis starts work on his seventh film, *Wild in the Country*.

November 23: Elvis releases his first gospel album, *His Hand in Mine*. Side 1 consists of "His Hand in Mine," "I'm Gonna Walk Dem Golden Stairs," "In My Father's House," "Milky White Way," "Known Only to Him," and "I Believe in the Man in the Sky." Side 2 consists of "Joshua Fit the Battle," "He Knows Just What I Need," "Swing Down, Sweet Chariot," "Mansion over the Hilltop," "If We Never Meet Again," and "Working on the Building."

November 23: The movie *GI Blues* opens to good reviews and sales.

Flaming Star

Based on the book *Flaming Lance* (1958) by Clair Huffaker. Critics agreed that Elvis gave one of his best acting performances as Pacer Burton in a dramatic role.

Director	Don Siegel
Producer	David Weisbart
Written by	Clair Huffaker, Nunnally Johnson
Starring	Elvis Presley, Barbara Eden, Dolores del Río
Music by	Cyril J. Mockridge
Cinematography	Charles G. Clarke
Editing by	Hugh S. Fowler
Distributed by	20th Century Fox
Release date	December 20, 1960 (USA)

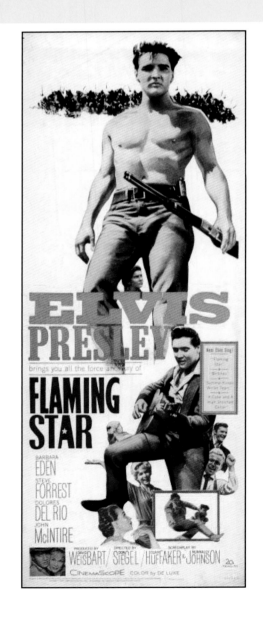

Elvis in Flaming Star, *1960*

December 22: The movie *Flaming Star* opens to warm reviews, but the box office figures aren't as good as those of *GI Blues* released one month earlier.

1961

January: Colonel Parker and Paramount negotiate a five-movie deal. Elvis gets $175,000 for the first three, $200,000 for the final pair. A bonus of $90,000 is added to the last movie, *Paradise, Hawaiian Style*. The same month Parker agrees to a four-movie deal with MGM, for which Elvis will get $500,000 in salary and expenses and 50% of the net profits.

January: Elvis achieves his sixth U.K. #1 hit with "Are You Lonesome Tonight?"

January 11: At a press conference, Colonel Parker announces a charity concert for the USS Arizona memorial.

February 13: "Surrender" and "Lonely Man" are released. Another platinum seller, the single goes to #1 in U.S., U.K., Canada, Australia, Belgium, South Africa, and Sweden.

February 25: It's Elvis Presley Day in Memphis and after a glittering luncheon commemorating the 75 million records he has sold to date, Elvis performs twice at Ellis Auditorium bringing in a total of $51,612: $47,823 will be divided among Memphis-area charities and $3,789 for the Elvis Presley Youth Recreation Center in Tupelo, Mississippi.

March 14: Elvis flies to Los Angeles to start work on his ninth movie, *Blue Hawaii*. Hawaii became the 50th state in 1960 and the movie is viewed as an excellent way of popularizing it as a destination.

March 23: Elvis achieves his seventh U.K. #1 with "Wooden Heart," which was not yet released in the U.S.

March 25: Elvis performs at Bloch Arena in Pearl Harbor, Hawaii, to help fund the USS Arizona Memorial. He raises around $62,000 for the memorial.

Wild in the Country

About a troubled young man from a dysfunctional family who pursues a literary career.

Director	Philip Dunne
Producer	Jerry Wald
Screenplay by	Clifford Odets
Based on	*The Lost Country* by J. R. Salamanca
Starring	Elvis Presley, Hope Lange, Tuesday Weld, Millie Perkins
Music by	Kenyon Hopkins
Cinematography	William C. Mellor
Editing by	Dorothy Spencer
Studio	20th Century Fox
Release date	June 15, 1961 (USA)

98

1961 (cont.)

Early April: Elvis begins work on location for *Blue Hawaii*.

May 8: "I Feel So Bad" and "Wild in the Country" are released. The single reaches #5 and goes gold in the U.S. and #4 in the U.K.

May 23: Elvis finishes shooting *Blue Hawaii*.

June 17: Elvis' 13th album, *Something for Everybody*, is released. Side 1 includes "There's Always Me," "Give Me the Right," "It's a Sin," "Sentimental Me," "Starting Today," and "Gently." Side 2 includes "I'm Comin' Home," "In Your Arms," "Put the Blame on Me," "Judy," "I Want You with Me," and "I Slipped, I Stumbled, I Fell." Another #1 hit for three weeks, the album spends 25 weeks on the charts and is certified gold in 1999.

June: Elvis achieves his eighth U.K. #1 single with "Surrender."

June 22: The movie *Wild in the Country* opens nationally.

July 1: Elvis is due to be best man at Red West's wedding, but turns up late so Joe Esposito stands in.

July 6–August 28: Elvis works on his ninth movie, *Follow That Dream*, with location work in Crystal River, Florida.

August 14: "Little Sister" and "(Marie's the Name of) His Latest Flame" are released. The single only reaches #4 in the U.S., but goes to #1 in the U.K. and Canada.

Elvis and Joan Blackman in Blue Hawaii, *1961 (far right)*

Blue Hawaii

The movie opened at #2 in box office receipts for the week. Despite mixed reviews from critics, it finished as the 10th top-grossing movie of 1961.

Director	Norman Taurog Michael D. Moore (assistant)
Producer	Hal B. Wallis Paul Nathan (associate)
Screenplay by	Hal Kanter
Story by	Allan Weiss
Starring	Elvis Presley, Joan Blackman, Angela Lansbury
Music by	Joseph J. Lilley
Cinematography	Charles Lang, Jr.
Editing by	Terry O. Morse
Studio	Hal Wallis Productions
Distributed by	Paramount Pictures
Release date	November 22, 1961 (USA)

ECSTATIC ROMANCE...EXOTIC DANCES...EXCITING MUSIC IN THE WORLD'S LUSHEST PARADISE OF SONG!

ELVIS PRESLEY RIDES THE CREST OF THE WAVE IN **BLUE HAWAII**

HAL WALLIS

TECHNICOLOR

JOAN BLACKMAN · ANGELA LANSBURY · NANCY WALTERS · NORMAN TAUROG · HAL KANTER

Elvis in Jailhouse Rock, *1957*

Elvis in Jailhouse Rock, *1957*

1961 (cont.)

October 1: Elvis' 14th album, *Blue Hawaii*, is released. Side 1 is "Blue Hawaii," "Almost Always True," "Aloha-Oe," "No More," "Can't Help Falling in Love," "Rock-A-Hula Baby," and "Moonlight Swim." Side 2 is "Ku-u-i-po," "Ito Eats," "Slicin' Sand," "Hawaiian Sunset," "Beach Boy Blues," "Island of Love," and "Hawaiian Wedding Song." One of Elvis' most successful albums, *Blue Hawaii* spent 18 months on the charts, including 20 weeks at #1, second only to GI Blues, and 39 weeks in the top 10. It was certified three-times platinum in 2002. The album lost out at the Grammys to the soundtrack from *Breakfast at Tiffany's*.

October 21: A pet chimp—named Scatter—arrives at Graceland.

October 26: Elvis works on United Artists' *Kid Galahad*, his 10th movie, initially training with former welterweight champion Mushy Callahan for his role as the boxer Walter Gulick.

November: Elvis registers his ninth U.K. #1 with "(Marie's the Name of) His Latest Flame."

November 4: Elvis begins filming *Kid Galahad* in Idyllwild, California.

November 20: "Can't Help Falling in Love" and "Rock-A-Hula Baby" are released. The single reaches #2 in the U.S. and #1 in the U.K. (Elvis' 10th #1 there), Canada, and South Africa.

November 22: The movie *Blue Hawaii* is released. Although it has some great songs, it starts a formulaic approach to movie making that will result in some real stinkers over the years.

December 20: Elvis finishes work on *Kid Galahad* and flies to Las Vegas. He stays there from December 22 to January 29 because he doesn't want to stay at Graceland with Vernon and his new wife.

December 28: Vernon, Dee, and her children move out of Graceland to Memphis.

Follow That Dream

The movie was based on the 1959 novel *Pioneer, Go Home!* by Richard P. Powell. Producer Walter Mirisch liked the song "Follow That Dream" and retitled the picture.

Director	Gordon Douglas
Producer	Walter Mirisch
Written by	Richard P. Powell (novel) Charles Lederer (screenwriter)
Starring	Elvis Presley, Anne Helm, Arthur O'Connell
Music by	Hans J. Salter
Cinematography	Leo Tover
Editing by	William B. Murphy
Studio	Mirisch Company
Distributed by	United Artists
Release date(s)	April 11, 1962 (USA)

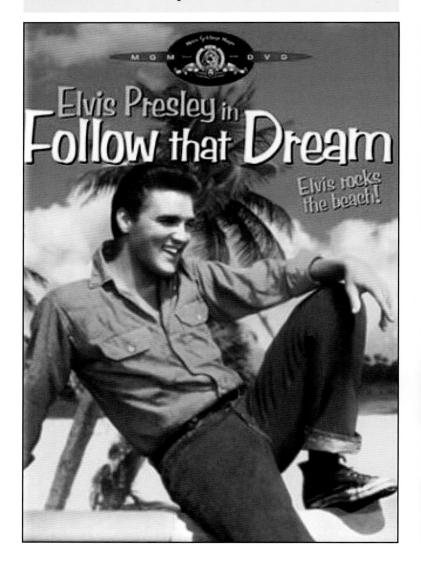

Elvis Presley, Anne Helm, Arthur O'Connell and the twins Gavin and Robin Koon in Follow That Dream *directed by Gordon Douglas [Mirisch Company], 1962*

THE KING REIGNS

March 10: "Good Luck Charm" and "Anything That's Part of You" are released. The single spends two weeks at #1 in the U.S.—Elvis will have to wait eight years for his next U.S. #1 hit—and reaches #1 in the U.K. (his 11th U.K. #1), Canada, Australia, Norway, South Africa, and Sweden.

March 26: Elvis begins work on his 11th movie, *Girls! Girls! Girls!* The soundtrack album will reach #3. Elvis insists "Return to Sender" is in the film. Good choice! It goes to #2.

April 7: Elvis arrives in Hawaii for filming and is mobbed at his hotel, losing some jewelry; his ring is returned the next day.

May 23: The movie *Follow That Dream* opens to good reviews.

June 5: *Pot Luck with Elvis*, his 15th album, is released. Side 1 includes "Kiss Me Quick," "Just for Old Time's Sake," "Gonna Get Back Home Somehow," "Easy Question," "Steppin' Out of Line," and "I'm Yours." Side 2 includes "Something Blue," "Suspicion," "I Feel That I've Known You Forever," "Night Rider," "Fountain of Love," and "That's Someone You Never Forget."

June 17–July 1: Priscilla, still living in Germany, visits Elvis. It is the first time the two have met for two years. He agrees to a set of rules with her family—and promptly disregards them. They go to Las Vegas and share a suite.

July 28: The new single "She's Not You" and "Just Tell Her Jim Said Hello" hits #1 in Ireland, Norway, and—for the 12th time—in the U.K.

August: Long-time girlfriend Anita Wood overhears Elvis talking about her and Priscilla. She leaves Elvis and Graceland.

August 28: Elvis starts his 12th movie, *It Happened at the World's Fair*. On September 4, location shooting takes place in Seattle.

August 29: The movie *Kid Galahad* opens.

October: The Mexican government bans Elvis movies after a showing of *GI Blues* leads to a riot.

Kid Galahad

Elvis plays the boxer Kid Galahad. Some critics rate it as one of Elvis' best performances. The film is a remake of the 1937 original starring Edward G. Robinson, Bette Davis, and Humphrey Bogart.

Director	Phil Karlson
Producer	David Weisbart
Written by	Francis Wallace William Fay
Starring	Elvis Presley, Lola Albright, Gig Young, Joan Blackman, Charles Bronson
Music by	Jeff Alexander
Cinematography	Burnett Guffey
Editing by	Stuart Gilmore
Studio	Mirisch Company
Distributed by	United Artists
Release date	August 11, 1962

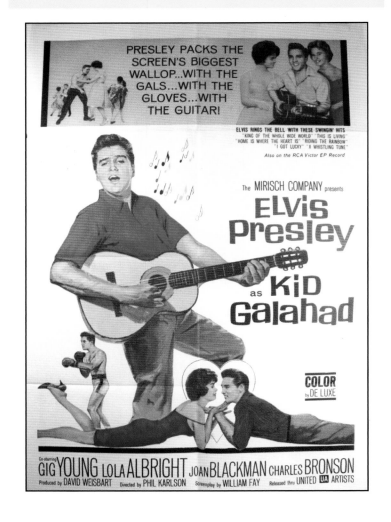

Elvis in a promotional shot for **Kid Galahad,** *1962*

October 13: "Return to Sender" and "Where Do You Come From?" are released. The single reaches #2 and is certified platinum. Abroad, it is Elvis' 14th U.K. #1 hit and reaches the top of the charts in Canada, Australia, Ireland, Norway, Spain, and Sweden.

November 21: The movie *Girls! Girls! Girls!* Opens. The soundtrack album is concurrently released. Side 1 includes "Girls! Girls! Girls!" "I Don't Wanna Be Tied," "Where Do You Come From?" "I Don't Want To," "We'll Be Together," "A Boy Like Me, A Girl Like You," and "Earth Boy." Side 2 includes "Return to Sender," "Because of Love," "Thanks to the Rolling Sea," "Song of the Shrimp," "The Walls Have Ears," and "We're Coming in Loaded."

December 19–January 11: Priscilla spends Christmas with Elvis in Memphis. Elvis gives her a toy poodle, which she names Honey.

1963

January 21–March 22: Elvis works on his 13th film, *Fun in Acapulco*.

Girls! Girls! Girls!

A musical comedy starring Elvis as a penniless Hawaiian fisherman who loves his life on the sea and dreams of owning his own boat. "Return to Sender," which reached #2 on the Billboard pop singles chart, is featured in the movie.

Director	Norman Taurog
Producer	Hal B. Wallis
Written by	Allan Weiss (story) Edward Anhalt
Starring	Elvis Presley, Stella Stevens, Laurel Goodwin
Music by	Joseph J. Lilley
Cinematography	Loyal Griggs
Editing by	Stanley E. Johnson
Studio	Hal Wallis Productions
Distributed by	Paramount Pictures
Release date	November 21, 1962 (USA)

Elvis in a promotional shot for Girls! Girls! Girls! *in 1962*

February 9: "One Broken Heart for Sale" and "They Remind Me Too Much of You" are released. The single goes gold, but only reaches #11. It sells best in Norway where it reaches #2.

March 2: Priscilla and her father stay in Graceland, where Captain Beaulieu succumbs to Elvis' charm offensive and agrees that Priscilla can enroll in the all-girl Immaculate Conception Cathedral High School. She does so and moves in with Vernon and Dee.

April 10: The movie *It Happened at the World's Fair* opens and the soundtrack album is released. Side 1 is "Beyond the Bend," "Relax," "Take Me to the Fair," "They Remind Me Too Much of You," and "One Broken Heart for Sale." Side 2 is "I'm Falling in Love Tonight," "Cotton Candy Land," "World of Our Own," "How Would You Like to Be?" and "Happy Ending." The album peaks at #4.

May 24: Priscilla celebrates her 18th birthday. She now lives in Graceland.

May 29: Elvis does not attend Priscilla's graduation ceremony at Immaculate Conception in case he provokes a riot.

July 9: Work starts on *Viva Las Vegas*, his 14th movie, which co-stars Ann-Margret with whom he will have a torrid affair.

July 27: When location shooting ends, Elvis returns to Los Angeles with Ann-Margret in tow. The romance becomes public in the press and Priscilla finds out.

June 29: "(You're the) Devil in Disguise" and "Please Don't Drag That String Around" are released. The single goes gold and reaches #3 in the U.S. It will reach #1 in the U.K., Canada, Belgium, France, Holland, Ireland, Norway, and Sweden.

August 15: Delays to *Viva Las Vegas* mean that Elvis' next movie, *Kissin' Cousins*, produced by MGM's Sam Katzman, will be released first. Filming of *Viva Las Vegas* ends on September 11.

It Happened at the World's Fair

A musical starring Elvis as a cropdusting pilot. It was filmed in Seattle, Washington, at the site of the Century 21 Exposition, also known as the 1962 World's Fair. The governor of Washington at the time, Albert Rosellini, suggested the setting to Metro-Goldwyn-Mayer executives.

Director	Norman Taurog
Producer	Ted Richmond
Written by	Si Rose Seaman Jacobs
Starring	Elvis Presley, Joan O'Brien, Gary Lockwood, Vicky Tiu
Music by	Leith Stevens
Cinematography	Joseph Ruttenberg
Editing by	Fredric Steinkamp
Studio	Ted Richmond Productions
Distributed by	Metro-Goldwyn-Mayer
Release date	April 3, 1963

Elvis and Gary Lockwood in It Happened at the World's Fair, *1963*

October: Elvis starts working on *Kissin' Cousins* with shooting finished on November 5.

October 12: The single "Bossa Nova Baby" and "Witchcraft" is released. The two songs are from the *Fun in Acapulco* movie soundtrack. The single reaches #8 on the Billboard Hot 100 and is certified gold. Abroad, it reaches the top in Belgium.

October 17: Elvis receives an honorary second-degree black belt in karate.

November: Colonel Parker agrees to a one-movie deal with Allied Artists for Elvis: $750,000 in salary and expenses and 50% of the profits. The film will be released in 1965 as *Tickle Me*.

Early November: The movie soundtrack *Fun in Acapulco* is released. Side 1 includes "Fun in Acapulco," "Vino, Dinero y Amor," "Mexico," "El Toro," "Marguerita," "The Bullfighter Was a Lady," and "(There's) No Room to Rhumba in a Sports Car." Side 2 includes "I Think I'm Gonna Like It Here," "Bossa Nova Baby," "You Can't Say No in Acapulco," "Guadalajara," "Love Me Tonight," and "Slowly But Surely."

November 6: Unnerved by the newspaper gossip about Elvis and Ann-Margret, Priscilla flies to Los Angeles. Elvis sends her home and is still with Ann-Margret on November 22 when President Kennedy is assassinated. Shortly thereafter, he returns to Priscilla and makes up.

November 27: The movie *Fun in Acapulco* opens and is immediately a box office hit. It becomes the top-grossing movie musical of 1963.

December 17: Elvis gives the mayor of Memphis $55,000 to be split among local charities. Also RCA extends Elvis' recording contract to 1971.

1964

February 9: Beatlemania hits the U.S. As Elvis did before, The Beatles make their mark when they appear on *The Ed Sullivan Show* in New York City. They receive a telegram: "Congratulations on your appearance on The Ed Sullivan Show and your visit to America. We hope your engagement will be a successful one and your visit pleasant. Please give our best to Mr. Sullivan, Sincerely Elvis & The Colonel."

Fun in Acapulco

Some exterior scenes were shot in Acapulco, Mexico, but Elvis scenes were shot in Hollywood. He never went to Acapulco. The movie featured the Top 10 Billboard hit "Bossa Nova Baby." The film reached #1 on the national weekly box office charts.

Director	Richard Thorpe
Producer	Hal B. Wallis
Written by	Allan Weiss
Starring	Elvis Presley, Ursula Andress, Paul Lukas, Elsa Cárdenas
Music by	Joseph J. Lilley
Cinematography	Daniel L. Fapp
Editing by	Stanley E. Johnson
Studio	Hal Wallis Productions
Distributed by	Paramount Pictures
Release date	November 27, 1963

1964 (cont.)

February 10: "Kissin' Cousins" and "It Hurts Me" are released. Not as successful as other singles, it still goes gold and reaches #11. Its best position worldwide is #2 in Denmark.

February 14: Elvis presents the *Potomac*, Franklin Delano Roosevelt's presidential yacht, bought at auction in January for $55,000, to St. Jude Children's Hospital in Memphis. It will be sold again and make $75,000 for the hospital.

February 17: Colonel Parker is hired as technical adviser for Elvis' 16th movie, *Roustabout*. Parker got his start on the carnival circuit, which is the subject of the film.

February 26–May 14: Elvis works on *Roustabout*. His co-star is Barbara Stanwyck.

March 6: The movie *Kissin' Cousins* opens nationally. It's a poor movie, but reaches #11 at the box office.

April 2: The album *Kissin' Cousins* is launched. It reaches #6. Side 1 includes "Kissin' Cousins" (a second version), "Smokey Mountain Boy," "There's Gold in the Mountains," "One Boy, Two Little Girls," "Catchin' on Fast," and "Tender Feeling." Side 2 includes "Anyone (Could Fall in Love with You)," "Barefoot Ballad," "Once Is Enough," "Kissin' Cousins," "Echoes of Love," and "Long Lonely Highway."

April 14: "Suspicion" and "Kiss Me Quick" are released. "Kiss Me Quick" reaches #34 in the U.S., but it does better internationally, reaching #2 in Belgium and #3 in Canada, Germany, Norway, and Sweden.

April 28: "Viva Las Vegas" and "What'd I Say" are released. Neither rises to higher than the #20s in the charts, before fading.

April 30: Elvis' usual hairdresser is unable to come to Elvis' home in the Bel-Air neighborhood of Los Angeles. Larry Geller is conscripted. They get on well, talking of "religion, spiritual growth, Elvis' early life, his mother and father, his twin brother, the church he attended in Tupelo and other very intimate subjects." Geller becomes his personal hairdresser and guru.

Kissin' Cousins

A comedy starring Elvis in two roles: one as an American soldier, the other a hillbilly. The screenplay was nominated in the category of best written American musical by the Writers Guild of America.

Director	Gene Nelson
Producer	Dick Fitzwell
Written by	Gerald Drayson Adams Gene Nelson
Starring	Elvis Presley, Yvonne Craig, Arthur O'Connell
Music by	Gene Nelson
Cinematography	Ellis W. Carter
Editing by	Ben Lewis
Studio	Four-Leaf Productions
Distributed by	Metro-Goldwyn-Mayer
Release date	March 6, 1964

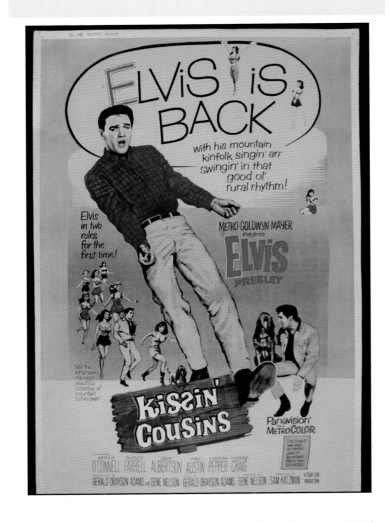

Elvis Presley in 1964

1964 (cont.)

June 9: Elvis starts work on his 17th film, *Girl Happy*, but hates the music. He gets on well with Mary Ann Mobley—a former Miss Mississippi and Miss America—who will also appear in an upcoming Elvis movie, Harum Scarum.

June 17: The movie *Viva Las Vegas* opens and goes to #14 at the box office. It's one of the better Elvis movies and will become Elvis' highest grossing film ever.

July 14: "Such a Night" and "Never Ending" are released. The single reaches #14 on the U.S. charts, but once again is more successful internationally, reaching #2 in Belgium and #3 in Australia.

August 17: Parker—after comments from his entourage—calls a meeting to discuss Elvis' "religious kick." Elvis gets angry and storms out.

September 21: Elvis becomes an official Special Deputy Sheriff for Shelby County.

Viva Las Vegas

A romantic musical regarded by fans and film critics alike as one of Elvis' best movies. It is noted for the on-screen chemistry between Elvis and Ann-Margret. It also presents a strong set of 10 musical song-and-dance scenes choreographed by David Winters and featuring his dancers.

Director	George Sidney
Producer	Jack Cummings George Sidney
Written by	Sally Benson
Starring	Elvis Presley, Ann-Margret
Music by	George E. Stoll
Cinematography	Joseph F. Biroc, ASC
Editing by	John McSweeney, Jr.
Studio	Jack Cummings Productions Winter Hollywood Entertainment Holdings Corporation
Distributed by	Metro-Goldwyn-Mayer
Release date	May 20, 1964

Elvis with Danny Thomas raising money for St. Jude's Childrens Hospital by auctioning FDR's yacht, Potomac, *donated by Elvis expressly to raise funds for the charity*

Elvis in Viva Las Vegas, *1964*

September 22: "Ain't That Lovin' You Baby?" (#1 in Spain) and "Ask Me" (#1 in Australia) are released. "Ask Me" reaches #11 in the U.S.

October 6: Elvis starts work on his 18th movie, *Tickle Me*. The soundtrack has no new recordings, using old material to keep production costs down.

October 20: *Roustabout*, Elvis' 21st album, is released. Side 1 is "Roustabout," "Little Egypt," "Poison Ivy League," "Hard Knocks," "It's a Wonderful World," and "Big Love, Big Heartache." Side 2 is "One Track Heart," "It's Carnival Time," "Carny Town," "There's a Brand New Day on the Horizon," and "Wheels on My Heels." Elvis would have to wait until 1973 for another soundtrack album to reach #1 on the Billboard charts. *Roustabout* was certified gold in 1988.

November: The movie *Roustabout* opens nationally and reaches #8 at the box office.

November 9: "Blue Christmas" and "Wooden Heart" are released, but are successful only in the U.K. where the single reaches #11 on the charts.

December: Colonel Parker renegotiates movie contracts with both United Artists and MGM. The deals, for two and three films, respectively, will earn Elvis $650,000 per UA film and $1million/$750,000/$750,000 for the MGM films plus 40% of the profits.

1965

January 8: Elvis celebrates his 30th birthday.

February 9: "Do the Clam" and "You'll Be Gone" are released. The single will go no higher than #21 in the U.S., but overseas it makes it to #2 in Denmark and #4 in Australia and Israel.

Early March: The soundtrack album from *Girl Happy* is released. It reaches #8 on the Billboard charts and goes gold in 1999. Side 1 includes "Girl Happy," "Spring Fever," "Fort Lauderdale Chamber of Commerce," "Startin' Tonight," "Wolf Call," and "Do Not Disturb." Side 2 includes "Cross My Heart and Hope to Die," "Meanest Girl in Town," "Do the Clam," "Puppet on a String," "I've Got to Find My Baby," and "You'll Be Gone."

Elvis in Viva Las Vegas, *1964*

1965 (cont.)

March 9–April 19: Elvis is at work on his next movie, *Harum Scarum*, including filming at the famous Iverson Film Ranch.

March 17: Elvis joins the Self-Realization Fellowship, led by Sri Daya Mata. Elvis will rely on him for spiritual guidance for the rest of his life.

April 4: After seeing Jerry Schilling's new Triumph motorcycle, Elvis buys one for himself— and for every member of the "Memphis Mafia," the group of friends, associates, employees, and "yes" men who hung out with the King.

April 6: "Crying in the Chapel" and "I Believe in the Man in the Sky" are released. The single makes it to #3 in the U.S., but climbs to #1 in the UK (Elvis' 15th U.K. #1 hit), Canada, Australia, Ireland, Norway, South Africa, Spain, and Israel.

April 7: The movie *Girl Happy* opens and is the 25th top-grossing film of the year.

May: Elvis starts work on his 20th movie, *Frankie and Johnny*, co-starring Donna Douglas. He is clearly angered by the songs and storms out of the studio on one occasion.

June 24: Elvis donates $50,000 to the Motion Picture Relief Fund. Barbara Stanwyck and Frank Sinatra accept for the fund.

July 7: The movie *Tickle Me* opens nationally and its success, while not huge, saves the Allied Artists studio from ruin.

August 2: Elvis begins recording the music for his 21st movie, *Paradise, Hawaiian Style*, and then goes to Hawaii for location shooting.

August 10: "I'm Yours" and "(It's a) Long, Lonely Highway" are released. The single goes to #11, but makes it to #2 in Canada.

August 15: During a break in filming, Elvis, Vernon, and Parker visit the USS Arizona Memorial, to which Elvis had donated the proceeds of a 1961 benefit concert.

Roustabout

A musical starring Elvis as a singer who takes a job working with a struggling carnival. The screenplay was nominated for a Writers Guild of America award although the movie received a lukewarm review in *Variety*. The film's soundtrack album was one of Elvis' most successful, reaching #1 on the Billboard Album Chart.

Director	John Rich
Producer	Hal B. Wallis
Written by	Allan Weiss
Screenplay:	Anthony Lawrence, Allan Weiss
Starring	Elvis Presley, Barbara Stanwyck, Joan Freeman, Leif Erickson
Music by	Joseph J. Lilley
Cinematography	Lucien Ballard
Editing by	Hal Pereira, Walter H. Tyler
Studio	Hal Wallis Productions
Distributed by	Paramount Pictures
Release date	November 11, 1964

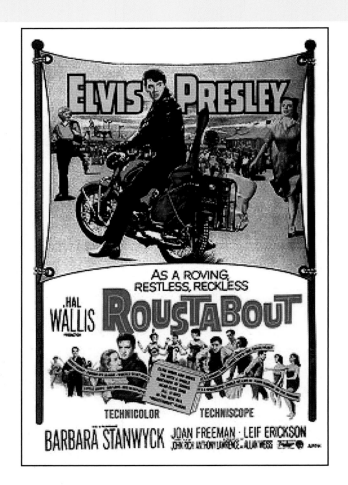

Elvis in Roustabout, *1964*

1965 (cont.)

August 27: The Beatles visit Elvis at his home on Perugia Way in the Bel-Air neighborhood of Los Angeles. No photography is allowed and no recordings are made of the jam session that ensues. As John Lennon leaves, he tells Jerry Schilling to make sure Elvis knows that "if it hadn't been for him, The Beatles would be nothing."

October 7: Graceland's Meditation Garden, inspired by the Self-Realization group's park, is finished.

October 8: *Elvis for Everyone* is released. The album contains a number of old, unreleased tracks and reaches #10. Side 1 is "Your Cheatin' Heart," "Summer Kisses, Winter Tears," "Finders Keepers, Losers Weepers," "In My Way," "Tomorrow Night," and "Memphis, Tennessee." Side 2 is "For the Millionth and Last Time," "Forget Me Never," "Sound Advice," "Santa Lucia," "I Met Her Today," and "When It Rains, It Really Pours."

October 20: "Puppet on a String" and "Wooden Heart" are released (with the latter being a re-release), and the single peaks at #14 on the charts.

October 21: Bill Black dies of a brain tumor at Memphis' Baptist Hospital.

October 22: Colonel Parker gets Elvis' RCA contract extended to 1972, despite poor recent sales.

October 26: "Santa Claus Is Back in Town" and "Blue Christmas" are released just before the holiday season. The single reaches #4 on the Christmas chart.

November 3: The *Harum Scarum* movie soundtrack is released. The album peaks at #8. Side 1 comprises "Harum Holiday," "My Desert Serenade," "Go East, Young Man," "Mirage," "Kismet," and "Shake That Tambourine." Side 2 comprises "Hey Little Girl," "Golden Coins," "So Close Yet So Far (from Paradise)," "Animal Instinct," and "Wisdom of the Ages."

Girl Happy

A beach-party film, spring-break style, *Girl Happy* is Elvis' 18th feature, was his last mega success at the box office. It finished #25 in the *Variety* year-end top-grossing films of 1965.

Director	Boris Sagal Jack Aldworth (assistant)
Producer	Joe Pasternak
Written by	Harvey Bullock R. S. Allen
Starring	Elvis Presley Shelley Fabares
Music by	George E. Stoll
Cinematography	Philip H. Lathrop
Editing by	Rita Roland Studio Euterpe
Distributed by	Metro-Goldwyn-Mayer
Release date	April 7, 1965

Elvis dances on the beach in Girl Happy, *1965*

November 24: The movie *Harum Scarum* opens nationally and reaches #11 at the box office.

December 3: "Tell Me Why" and "Blue River" are released, but go nowhere. "Tell Me Why" was actually recorded in 1957.

December 25: Priscilla gives Elvis a slot-car racetrack. The Memphis Mafia gives him a statue of Jesus for the Meditation Garden, and it's still there.

1966

January: MGM extends Elvis' contract for four more movies. For each, Elvis will receive $850,000 and 50% of the profits.

February 1–April 8: Elvis films his 22nd movie, *Spinout*, co-starring Shelley Fabares.

February 15: After "Crying in the Chapel" was a huge hit in 1965, RCA issued more gospel singles by Elvis at Easter for the next seven years. The two singles released in 1966 are "Joshua Fit the Battle" and "Known Only to Him," and "Milky White Way" and "Swing Down, Sweet Chariot."

April: Colonel Parker and Hal Wallis of Warner Brothers start what will be seven months of debate over contract details. In the end, an agreement ($500,000 and 20% of the profits) is made for one film—*Easy Come, Easy Go*.

March 1: RCA has a double release of the single "Frankie and Johnny" and "Please Don't Stop Loving Me" and the soundtrack album for the movie *Frankie and Johnny*. Side 1 includes "Frankie and Johnny," "Come Along," "Petunia, the Gardener's Daughter," "Chesay," "What Every Woman Lives For," and "Look Out Broadway." Side 2 includes "Beginner's Luck," "Down by the Riverside/When the Saints Go Marching In," "Shout It Out," "Hard Luck," "Please Don't Stop Loving Me," and "Everybody Come Aboard." The single will peak at #25 and the album at #20.

Tickle Me

A Western musical in which Elvis stars as a champion rodeo bull-rider and bronco-buster. Elvis won a 1966 Golden Laurel Award as the best male actor in a musical film for his role in this comedy. It is also the only Elvis film released by Allied Artists Pictures. It single-handedly saved the Allied Artists studio from financial collapse

Director	Norman Taurog Arthur Jacobson
Producer	Ben Schwalb
Written by	Elwood Ullman Edward Bernds
Starring	Elvis Presley, Julie Adams, Jocelyn Lane
Music by	Walter Scharf
Cinematography	Loyal Griggs
Editing by	Archie Marshek
Distributed by	Allied Artists Pictures Corporation
Release date	June 30, 1965

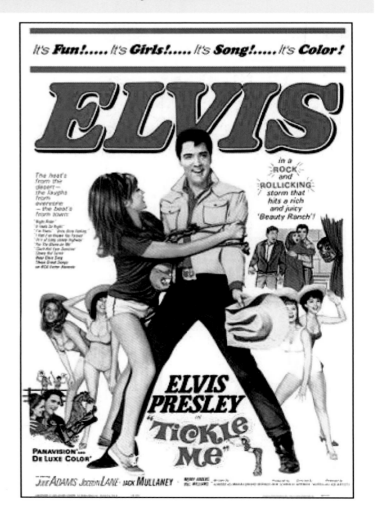

Elvis in the Western Tickle Me, *1965*

1966 (cont.)

May 25: Elvis meets record producer Felton Jarvis and starts on the gospel album *How Great Thou Art*.

June–September: Elvis works on his 23rd movie, *Double Trouble*. Set in Europe, but filmed in Hollywood, it's bland and—embarrassingly—Elvis has to sing "Old McDonald Had a Farm."

June 10: The soundtrack to the movie *Paradise, Hawaiian Style* is released, and surprisingly, considering its mediocre fare, peaks at #15. Side 1 comprises "Paradise, Hawaiian Style," "Queenie Wahine's Papaya," "Scratch My Back," "Drums of the Islands," and "Datin'." Side 2 comprises "Dog's Life," "House of Sand," "Stop Where You Are," "This Is My Heaven," and "Sand Castles."

July 6: The movie *Paradise, Hawaiian Style* is released, making it only to #40 at the box office for the year. The soundtrack album peaks at #15.

June 8: "Love Letters" and "Come What May" are released. The single will reach #19 on the charts. The days of Elvis' #1 singles seem a long way away.

August 30: Deciding not to wait until the end of 1967, RCA picks up its option to extend Elvis' contract until 1974.

September–November: Elvis works on his next movie, *Easy Come, Easy Go*. What could have been a witty take on Flower Power and hippiedom will prove to be banal and trite.

September 13: "Spinout" and "All That I Am" are released. Until late 1969, none of Elvis' future singles will get into the Billboard top 10.

September 21: Elvis signs a lease on a Palm Springs, California, house at 1350 Ladera Circle.

October 31: The *Spinout* soundtrack is released ahead of the movie. Side 1 includes "Stop, Look, and Listen," "Adam and Evil," "Never Say Yes," "Am I Ready?" and "Beach Shack." Side 2 includes "Spinout," "Smorgasbord," "I'll Be Back," "Tomorrow Is a Long Time," "Down in the Alley," and "I'll Remember You." The soundtrack album goes to #18.

Harum Scarum

A musical comedy shot on the original Cecil B. DeMille set from the film *The King of Kings*. Some of the film was based on Rudolph Valentino's *The Sheik*, which was released in 1921.

Director	Gene Nelson
Producer	Sam Katzman
Written by	Elwood Ullman Edward Bernds
Starring	Elvis Presley, Mary Ann Mobley
Music by	Fred Karger
Cinematography	Fred Jackman Jr.
Editing by	Ben Lewis
Studio	Four-Leaf Productions
Distributed by	Metro-Goldwyn-Mayer
Release date	November 24, 1965

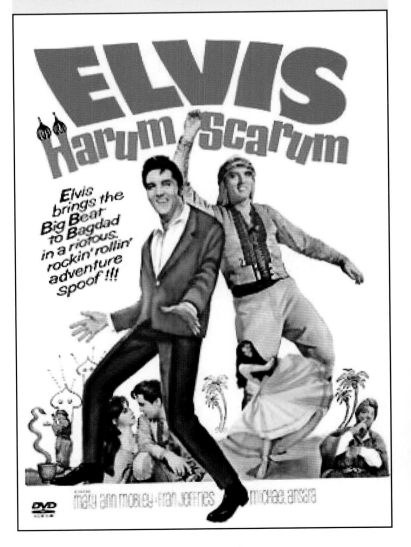

Elvis in Harum Scarum, *1965*

November 15: The single "If Everyday Was Like Christmas" and "How Would You Like to Be?" reaches #9 in the U.K.

November 23: The movie *Spinout* opens nationally and is one of Elvis' better mid–1960s films. It's funny and engaging.

December 12: As usual, Elvis makes a significant donation to Memphis charities, this year $105,000 in total.

December 20: Elvis buys horses for Priscilla (a black Tennessee walking horse named Domino) and for Jerry Schilling's fiancée, Sandy Kawelo (Sheba). He will later buy a palomino named Rising Sun that will be housed in stables named House of the Rising Sun!

December 24: Elvis finally goes down on one knee during Christmas celebrations and gives Priscilla a ring, saying, "We're going to be married."

1967

January 2: Colonel Parker renegotiates his arrangement with Elvis, upping his share of the profits from 25% to 50%.

January 10: "Indescribably Blue" and "Fools Fall in Love" are released as a single.

January 15: When Vernon's sister, Delta, is widowed, Elvis invites her to live at Graceland. She will do so until her death in 1993.

January 24: Colonel Parker again renegotiates Elvis' contract with RCA through 1974. As was usual, the main beneficiary was Parker.

February 8: Elvis buys the Twinkletown Farm horse ranch, christening it the Circle G, for Graceland. Twinkletown Farm is 163 acres, is minutes from Graceland, and costs $437,000.

February 20: Elvis' second gospel album, *How Great Thou Art*, is released and will win Elvis the first of his three Grammys. It reaches #18 in the charts. Side 1 is "How Great Thou Art," "In the Garden," "Somebody Bigger Than You and I," "Farther Along," "Stand By Me," and "Without

Frankie and Johnny

Musical film starring Elvis Presley as a riverboat gambler. The role of Frankie was played by Donna Douglas from *The Beverly Hillbillies* TV series.

Director	Frederick de Cordova
Producer	Edward Small
Written by	Nat Perrin Alex Gottlieb
Starring	Elvis Presley, Donna Douglas, Harry Morgan
Music by	Fred Karger
Cinematography	Jacques R. Marquette
Editing by	Grant Whytock
Studio	Edward Small Productions
Distributed by	United Artists
Release date	March 31, 1966

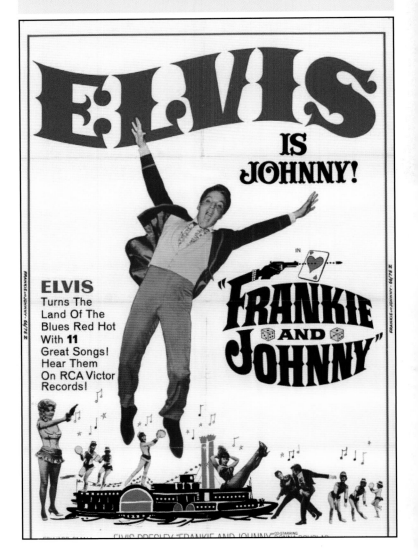

1967 (cont.)

Him." Side 2 is "So High," "Where Could I Go But to the Lord?" "By and By," "If the Lord Wasn't Walking by My Side," "Run On," "Where No One Stands Alone," and "Crying in the Chapel."

February 26: Elvis delays his trip to Hollywood to start filming *Clambake* because he has saddle sores. Dr. George Nichopoulos helps and begins a professional involvement that would last until Elvis' death.

March–April: Elvis works on *Clambake*, his third movie with co-star Shelley Fabares, and it's another forgettable movie.

March 22: Filming on *Clambake* begins on the same day the movie *Easy Come, Easy Go* premieres in San Francisco. It is supported by an EP (extended play) soundtrack, released in May, which doesn't sell well and is Elvis' last EP recording.

April 5: The film *Double Trouble* opens nationally. Although better than some of his recent screen efforts, it ranks #58 at the box office for the year.

April 28: "Long-Legged Girl (With the Short Dress On)" and "That's Someone You Never Forget" are released.

May 1: Elvis and Priscilla are married at the Aladdin hotel in Las Vegas. The two best men are Joe Esposito and Marty Lacker. The night before, they stay at 1350 Ladera Circle in Palm Springs, California, in a house Elvis leased. They depart early in the morning for Las Vegas and return to Palm Springs after the wedding.

May 24: Priscilla celebrates her 22nd birthday.

May 29: Elvis and Priscilla don their wedding clothes again and have a second reception for family and friends who were not in Las Vegas for the wedding.

Paradise, Hawaiian Style

Another musical comedy for Elvis. It was the third and final motion picture that Elvis filmed in Hawaii. The film reached #40 on the *Variety* weekly box office chart, earning $2.5 million in theaters.

Director	Michael D. Moore
Producer	Hal B. Wallis
Written by	Anthony Lawrence Allan Weiss
Starring	Elvis Presley, Suzanna Leigh, James Shigeta
Cinematography	W. Wallace Kelley
Editing by	Warren Low
Studio	Hal Wallis Productions
Distributed by	Paramount Pictures
Release date	June 9, 1966

A publicity shot for Paradise, Hawaiian Style, *1966*

1967 (cont.)

June 1: The soundtrack album from *Double Trouble* is released. The album is Elvis' lowest charting to date. Side 1 is "Double Trouble," "Baby If You'll Give Me All of Your Love," "Could I Fall in Love?" "Long-Legged Girl (with the Short Dress On)," "City by Night," and "Old MacDonald." Side 2 is "I Love Only One Girl," "There Is So Much World to See," "It Won't Be Long," "Never Ending," "Blue River," and "What Now, What Next, Where To."

June 7: Ann-Margret opens in Las Vegas. Elvis sends her congratulatory flowers.

June 9: Priscilla finds out she is pregnant.

June–August: Elvis works on *Speedway*, co-starring Nancy Sinatra. Roger Ebert of the *Chicago Sun-Times* calls it "pleasant, kind, polite, sweet and noble."

July 12: Priscilla's pregnancy is made public. Elvis says, "This is the greatest thing that has ever happened to me."

August 8: "There's Always Me" and "Judy" are released.

September 26: "Big Boss Man" and "You Don't Know Me" are released.

September 29: Memphis Mayor William Ingram and Tennessee Governor Buford Ellington declare Elvis Presley Day in recognition of his charitable contributions. Elvis names one of his horses Mare Ingram in the mayor's honor.

October–November: Elvis works on the Western comedy *Stay Away Joe*.

October 10: The *Clambake* soundtrack album is released. Another low-charting record, selling fewer than 200,000 copies, it reaches #40. Side 1 is "Guitar Man," "Clambake," "Who Needs Money?" "A House That Has Everything," "Confidence," and "Hey, Hey, Hey." Side 2 is "You Don't Know Me," "The Girl I Never Loved," "How Can You Lose What You Never Had?" "Big Boss Man," "Singing Tree," and "Just Call Me Lonesome."

Spinout

Mike McCoy (Elvis), the lead singer for a traveling band who is also a part-time race car driver, enjoys his carefree single life, which is being threatened by three different women who seek to marry him.

Director	Norman Taurog James A. Rosenberger
Producer	Joe Pasternak
Written by	Theodore J. Flicker & George Kirgo
Starring	Elvis Presley Shelley Fabares
Music by	George Stoll & various
Cinematography	Daniel L. Fapp
Editing by	Rita Roland
Distributed by	MGM
Release date(s)	October 17, 1966

October 18: Elvis' last United Artists movie, *Clambake*—for which he receives a million dollars—premieres. It is released nationally in December and goes to #15 at the box office, but not good enough for a seven-figure fee, as the critics point out.

November: Parker negotiates a one-film deal with National General. Elvis will get $850,000 and 50% of the profits. Remarkably, he won't sing in the movie *Charro!*

November: Elvis and Priscilla buy a home at 1174 Hillcrest in Beverly Hills, California, for $400,000. It's a three-bedroomed house with an Olympic-sized swimming pool. They won't live there until late February.

November 6: Colonel Parker starts negotiations with NBC for a 1968 Christmas TV special.

1968

January 9: "Guitar Man" and "High Heel Sneakers" are released. Although unsuccessful now (it peaks at #43), in 1981 an electric remix of this Jerry Reed song will take Elvis to a posthumous #1 on the Billboard Country chart.

January 12: Colonel Parker and NBC vice president Tom Sarnoff announce the Elvis Christmas TV Special—it will be the first time in eight years that he has appeared on TV and—against Parker's better judgment—in seven years in front of a live audience. It will earn him $250,000 with a linked movie deal worth $850,000.

February 1: At Memphis' Baptist Hospital at 5:01 p.m., Priscilla gives birth to Lisa Marie nine months to the day after the marriage. The baby weighs 6 lbs. 15 oz.

February 25: Elvis and his family move to their new home at 1174 Hillcrest in Los Angeles.

February 28: "U.S. Male" and "Stay Away" are released.

February 29: At the Tenth Grammy Awards, Elvis wins a Grammy for Best Sacred Performance with "How Great Thou Art."

Easy Come, Easy Go

Elvis plays a former U.S. Navy frogman who divides his time between twin careers as a deep-sea diver and nightclub singer. Ted discovers what he believes could be a fortune in Spanish gold aboard a sunken ship and sets out to rescue it with the help of a go-go dancing yoga expert. Someone else is also after the treasure and a race ensues.

Director	John Rich Robert Goodstein
Producer	Hal B. Wallis
Written by	Allan Weiss Anthony Lawrence
Starring	Elvis Presley Pat Priest
Music by	Joseph J. Lilley
Cinematography	William Margulies
Editing by	Archie Marshek
Distributed by	Paramount Pictures
Release date	March 22, 1967

Elvis in Easy Come, Easy Go, *1967*

1968 (cont.)

March 8: The film *Stay Away Joe* opens to mixed reviews and is #65 at the box office for the year.

March–May: Elvis works on *Live a Little, Love a Little*—a more mature film with fewer songs, featuring cameos of Vernon Presley, "Red" West, Joe Esposito, and Elvis' Great Dane, Brutus.

March 26: "You'll Never Walk Alone" and "We Call on Him" are released.

May 1: *Speedway*, Elvis' 32nd album and another movie soundtrack, is released on the heels of The Beatles' *Sgt. Pepper* album. Its sales are poor even after the film of the same name appears in June. Side 1 comprises "Speedway," "There Ain't Nothing Like a Song," "Your Time Hasn't Come Yet, Baby," "Who Are You? (Who Am I?)," "He's Your Uncle, Not Your Dad," and "Let Yourself Go." Side 2 comprises "Your Groovy Self," "Five Sleepy Heads," "Western Union," "Mine," "Goin' Home," and "Suppose."

May 17: Steve Binder is hired as director for Elvis' Christmas TV special.

May 21: "Let Yourself Go" and "Your Time Hasn't Come Yet Baby" are released.

May 25: Priscilla and Elvis watch a karate tournament in Hawaii. They meet Mike Stone, with whom Priscilla will have the affair that leads to their divorce.

June: Elvis works on the Christmas TV Special with Scotty, D.J., Alan Fortas, Lance LeGault, and his old friend, Charlie Hodge. Hodge met Elvis in 1955 when he was a singer with The Foggy River Boys gospel band and then again in 1958 at Fort Hood in Arkansas. As part of the Memphis Mafia, he was Elvis' stage manager when he returned to touring and also was a close friend. There are a number of segments to the show: a seated jam session, a gospel medley, a bordello section, and a stand-up session.

June 11: Elvis meets the costume director for the NBC TV Christmas special, Bill Belew. The relationship will continue for the rest of Elvis' working life. Belew will design the jumpsuits of the 1970s.

Double Trouble

When singer Guy Lambert, played by Elvis, tours Europe, he is pursued by two beautiful women, bumbling jewel thieves, and a mysterious killer.

Director	Norman Taurog Robert Goodstein (assistant)
Producer	Irwin Winkler Judd Bernard
Written by	Mark Brandel Jo Heims
Starring	Elvis Presley, Annette Day, John Williams
Music by	Jeff Alexander
Cinematography	Daniel L. Fapp
Editing by	John McSweeney, Jr.
Distributed by	MGM
Release date	April 5, 1967

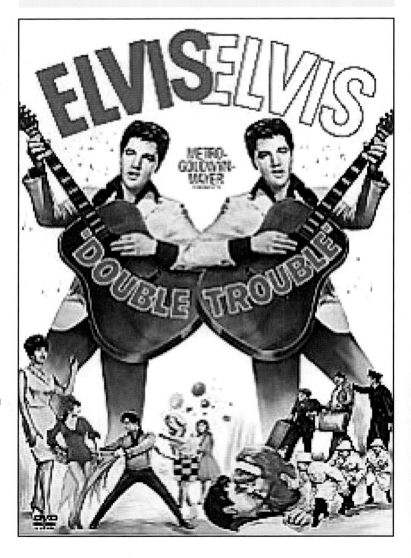

Elvis as singer Guy Lambert in
Double Trouble, *1967*

1968 (cont.)

June 12: *Speedway*, the movie, is released and reaches #40 at the box office for the year.

June 17: Rehearsals begin for the Christmas TV special.

June 27: The rehearsals over, the filming begins. Elvis and his band perform two jam sessions on NBC's center stage in the afternoon and evening.

June 28: The gospel portion and the controversial bordello scene are filmed—the latter isn't broadcast because the sponsor, Singer Sewing Machines, thinks it might upset viewers.

June 29: The introduction and two stand-up musical sets are filmed in front of a packed house.

June 30: The finale, the inspirational "If I Can Dream," specially written by Earl Brown, is taped in five takes.

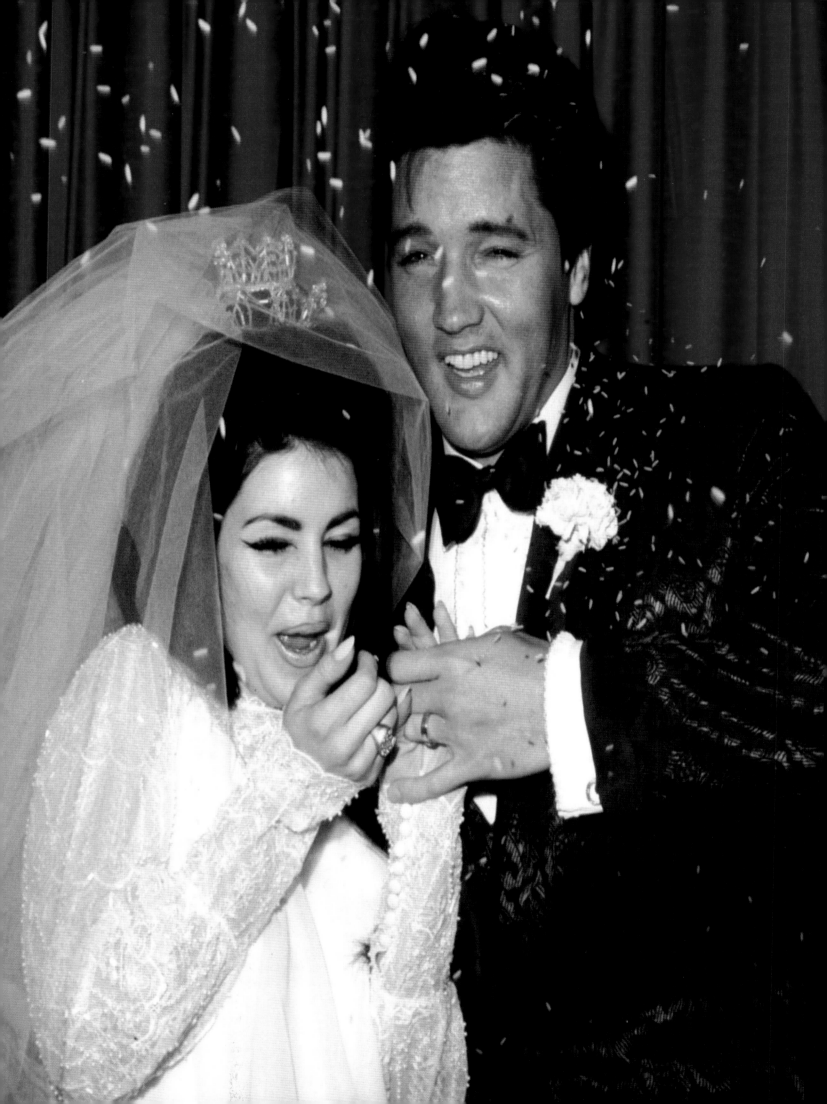

Priscilla shows off her wedding band (above) and she and Elvis cut their wedding cake (right) at the Aladdin Hotel in Las Vegas on their wedding day, May 1, 1967. They would have another reception later to celebrate with family and friends who could not attend the wedding.

Priscilla, 21 years old, and Elvis pose for their official wedding photo with their wedding party.

On their honeymoon, Elvis and Priscilla prepare to board a private plane, May 1967.

*Elvis and Priscilla spent their honeymoon in this house at
1350 Ladera Circle in Palm Springs, California.*

And baby makes three when Lisa Marie is born on February 1, 1968.

Elvis, Priscilla, and Lisa Marie relax by the pool at Graceland in Memphis (above), and Elvis plays with Lisa Marie (right).

Lisa Marie dressed in white fur (below)

1968 (cont.)

July–August: Elvis works on his 29th movie, the western *Charro!* It is a departure from the previous style of films Elvis has made. He's bearded and only sings the title song. It doesn't catch the public's imagination.

August 20: Colonel Parker previews the Christmas TV special and forces NBC to re-insert "Blue Christmas" from the sit-down show that had been edited out.

September 3: "A Little Less Conversation" and "Almost in Love" are released. Although of little interest to a 1968 audience, the 2001 remix of "A Little Less Conversation" topped the charts at #1.

October–December 18: Elvis works on his 30th movie, *The Trouble with Girls.* Unlike *Charro!* Elvis performs a number of songs consistent with the Elvis formula.

Elvis and Priscilla enjoy a private joke as Lisa Marie plays peek-a-boo (above), and the Presley girls celebrate Lisa Marie's fifth birthday on February 1, 1973, in matching mother/daughter dresses while Elvis looks on.

The King and his queen in the early 1970s

Elvis in his NBC Christmas special that aired December 3, 1968

Elvis in his NBC Christmas special that aired December 3, 1968

Tom Jones, Priscilla, and Elvis on April 6, 1968

1968 (cont.)

October 1: Elvis attends the funeral of Dewey Phillips, the influential disc jockey who'd been the first to play his debut record, "That's All Right Mama."

October: *Singer Presents Elvis Singing Flaming Star and Others* is released. This promotional tie-in with the Christmas TV special is available at stores selling Singer products before it goes into general release in March 1969. Although the album only reaches #96 on the charts in the U.S., it reaches #2 in the U.K. and will be certified platinum in 2004. Side 1 is "Flaming Star," "Wonderful World," "Night Life," "All I Needed Was the Rain," and "Too Much Monkey Business." Side 2 is "Yellow Rose of Texas/The Eyes of Texas," "She's a Machine," "Do the Vega," and "Tiger Man."

October 23: The MGM film *Live a Little, Love a Little* opens. It performs so badly it is not widely distributed.

November 5: "If I Can Dream" and "Edge of Reality" are released. The single peaks at #12—much better than recent singles and Elvis' highest chart position since 1965.

November 22: The album *Elvis NBC-TV Special '68 Comeback!* is released. It is an enormous success reaching #8 in the U.S., #2 in the U.K., and #4 in Canada and will be certified platinum. This—in conjunction with the TV show—resuscitates Elvis' career. Side 1 is "Trouble/Guitar Man," "Lawdy Miss Clawdy/Baby What You Want Me to Do?" and a medley of "Heartbreak Hotel/Hound Dog/All Shook Up/Can't Help Falling in Love/Jailhouse Rock/Love Me Tender." Side 2 is a medley of "Where Could I Go But to the Lord?/Up Above My Head/Saved," "Blue Christmas," "One Night," "Memories," "Nothingville/Big Boss Man/Guitar Man/Little Egypt/Trouble/Guitar Man," and "If I Can Dream."

Elvis Presley in 1969

December 3: The NBC TV special, *Singer Presents Elvis*, starts at 9 p.m. EST and is a huge success. From his informal jam with Scotty, D.J., and friends to the gospel section backed by the female vocal group The Blossoms, to his solo finale singing "If I Can Dream," leather-clad, lighter than he's been for a while, Elvis is brilliant.

1969

January 6: Marty Lacker suggests that Elvis should work with producer Chips Moman at American Sound Studio.

January 13: Elvis has his first session at American Sound, and he loves it.

January 22: Elvis records a song that his new producer, Chips Moman, has acquired for him, "Suspicious Minds."

February 1: Lisa Marie's first birthday is spent in Aspen, Colorado.

February 25: "Memories" and "Charro" are released. The single reaches #35.

March–April: Elvis works on his 31st—and last— movie, *Change of Habit*, co-starring Mary Tyler Moore.

March 13: The film *Charro!* opens in theaters and doesn't do much at the box office.

March 25: "His Hand in Mine" and "How Great Thou Art" are released. Although the single will do little in the pop charts, Elvis will win a Grammy in 1974 for Best Inspirational Performance (Non-Classical) for a live version of "How Great Thou Art" that appeared on his album, *Recorded Live on Stage in Memphis*.

April: "In the Ghetto" and "Any Day Now" are released and will be Elvis' best selling single for many years. It reaches #3 in the U.S., #2 in the U.K. and Canada, and #1 in Australia, Belgium, Ireland, New Zealand, Norway, Spain, and Sweden.

Clambake

The son of an extremely rich oil tycoon rebels against the plans and expectations of his father. The son, played by Elvis, abandons his family, driving to Florida in his shiny red Corvette to find himself.

Director	Arthur H. Nadel
Producer	Arthur Gardner Arnold Laven Jules Levy
Written by	Arthur Browne, Jr.
Starring	Elvis Presley, Will Hutchins, Shelley Fabares, Bill Bixby
Music by	Jeff Alexander
Cinematography	William Margulies
Editing by	Tom Rolf
Studio	Levy-Gardner-Laven Rhodes Pictures
Distributed by	United Artists
Release date	October 18, 1967

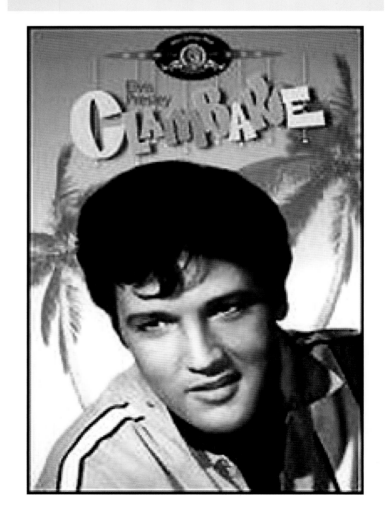

1969 (cont.)

June 17: Elvis' 35th album, *From Elvis in Memphis*, the result of his sessions at the American Sound Studio, is released. Much of the material is held back and saved for the double album *From Memphis to Vegas/From Vegas to Memphis* that will be released later in the year. Side 1 is "Wearin' That Loved-On Look," "Only the Strong Survive," "I'll Hold You in My Heart (Till I Can Hold You in My Arms)," "Long Black Limousine," "It Keeps Right On A-Hurtin'," and "I'm Movin' On." Side 2 is "Power of My Love," "Gentle on My Mind," "After Loving You," "True Love Travels on a Gravel Road," "Any Day Now," and "In the Ghetto." The album reaches #13 in the U.S. and #1 in the U.K. and was certified gold in 1970. The single "Clean Up Your Own Back Yard" and "The Fair's Moving On" is released on the same day.

July 14: The band for Elvis' upcoming gig at the International Hotel in Las Vegas is put together by guitarist James Burton who hires Larry Muhoberac (piano), John Wilkinson (rhythm guitar), Jerry Scheff (bass), and Ronnie Tutt (drums). Elvis chooses the back-up vocalists: a male gospel quartet, the Imperials, and the all-girl Sweet Inspirations, who had backed Aretha Franklin. The orchestra is conducted by Bobby Morris. Rehearsals start on July 18.

July 31–August 28: Elvis' first appearance in Las Vegas starts at 10:15 p.m. with "Blue Suede Shoes." He wears a karate-style outfit designed by Bill Belew. It is an instant success, and the four-week engagement breaks Las Vegas attendance records. A critical triumph, it also leads to Elvis' first live album, *Elvis in Person at the International Hotel*. Elvis also receives a gold belt from the hotel for his championship attendance.

August 26: "Suspicious Minds" and "You'll Think of Me" provide Elvis' first #1 single since "Good Luck Charm" in 1962. It will also be his last #1 single in the Billboard Hot 100 in his lifetime. Around the world the single is a huge success, ensuring it goes platinum. It reaches #2 in the U.K. and #1 in Canada, Australia, Belgium, New Zealand, and South Africa.

Stay Away Joe

Elvis stars as the Native American rodeo rider Joe Lightcloud, a Navajo whose family still lives on the reservation. He returns to the reservation in a white Cadillac convertible with which he proceeds to drive cattle.

Director	Peter Tewksbury Robert Goodstein
Producer	Douglas Laurence
Written by	Michael A. Hoey Burt Kennedy
Based on	*Stay Away, Joe* by Dan Cushman
Starring	Elvis Presley, Joan Blondell, Burgess Meredith
Music by	Jack Marshall
Cinematography	Fred J. Koenekamp
Editing by	George W. Brooks
Distributed by	MGM
Release date	March 8, 1968

September 3: Elvis' 30th movie, MGM's *The Trouble with Girls*, opens in theaters and isn't much of a success at the box office.

October 14: Elvis' 36th album, *From Memphis to Vegas/From Vegas to Memphis*, is released to acclaim. It will reach #12 and go gold in 1969. Side 1 of the double album includes "Blue Suede Shoes," "Johnny B. Goode," "All Shook Up," "Are You Lonesome Tonight?" "Hound Dog," "I Can't Stop Loving You," and "My Babe." Side 2 includes "Mystery Train/Tiger Man," "Words," "In the Ghetto," "Suspicious Minds," and "Can't Help Falling in Love." Side 3 includes "Inherit the Wind," "This Is the Story," "Stranger in My Own Home Town," "A Little Bit of Green," and "And the Grass Won't Pay No Mind." Side 4 includes "Do You Know Who I Am?" "From a Jack to a King," "The Fair's Moving On," "You'll Think of Me," and "Without Love (There Is Nothing)."

November 10: Elvis' last acting role in his 31st movie, *Change of Habit*, co-starring Mary Tyler Moore, premieres. It reaches a respectable #17 at the box office, but going forward Elvis will stick to live on-stage performing.

November 11: The single "Don't Cry Daddy" and "Rubberneckin'" reaches #6 in the U.S. and #8 in the U.K.

1970

January 26–February 23: Elvis returns to Las Vegas for another month-long engagement. Wearing a one-piece jumpsuit and incorporating karate moves into his stage show, the International Hotel attendance figures get better and better. A live album is recorded during this time and is released June 23.

January 29: "Kentucky Rain" and "My Little Friend" are released. The single goes gold and peaks at #16.

February 27: Elvis performs in his first-ever stadium show at the Houston Astrodome. He performs afternoon and evening, and again on February 28 and March 1. He is watched by 207,494 fans.

Speedway

A race car driver finds himself in deep trouble with the IRS because his winnings have been mismanaged and he owes back taxes. A female IRS agent is assigned to keep tabs on him and to ensure he applies his future winnings toward his $150,000 debt. She keeps a much closer eye on him than she anticipated.

Director	Norman Taurog Robert Goodstein (assistant)
Producer	Douglas Laurence
Written by	Phillip Shuke
Starring	Elvis Presley Nancy Sinatra Bill Bixby
Music by	Jeff Alexander
Cinematography	Joseph Ruttenberg
Editing by	Richard W. Farrell
Distributed by	MGM
Release date	June 12, 1968

Elvis and Nancy Sinatra in
Speedway, *1968*

1970 (cont.)

April: Colonel Parker negotiates a deal with MGM for a documentary on Elvis' Las Vegas show. Elvis receives $500,000. Elvis puts down a deposit on 845 Chino Canyon Road in Palm Springs, California. Elvis adds a swimming pool to the house, which was built in 1965. It will be sold in 1979 to Frankie Valli for $385,000.

April 1: Elvis' 37th album, *Let's Be Friends*, a collection of unpublished older songs, is released. It only reaches #101, but will be certified platinum in 2004. Side 1 is "Stay Away Joe," "If I'm a Fool (for Loving You)," "Let's Be Friends," "Let's Forget about the Stars," and "Mama." Side 2 is "I'll Be There," "Almost," "Change of Habit," and "Have a Happy."

April 20: The single "The Wonder of You" and "Mama Liked the Roses" reaches #9 in the U.S. and #1 in the U.K. and Ireland. It is Elvis' 16th U.K. #1 hit and stays on top of the charts for six weeks, selling 700,000 copies.

June 1: Felton Jarvis leaves RCA and signs an exclusive contract with Elvis. He will be his producer for the rest of Elvis' life. On June 4, he and Elvis enter RCA's Nashville studios and over a period of five nights record 34 songs, forming the basis for two more albums, *Elvis Country* and *Love Letters from Elvis*.

June 23: The live album recorded at the International Hotel in Las Vegas earlier in the year is released. *On Stage: February 1970* has sold over 10 million copies to date and was certified platinum in 1999. Side 1 is "See See Rider," "Release Me," "Sweet Caroline," "Runaway," "The Wonder of You," and "I'm Movin' On." Side 2 is "Polk Salad Annie," "Yesterday," "Proud Mary," "Walk a Mile in My Shoes," and "Let It Be Me."

July 14: "I've Lost You" and "The Next Step Is Love" are released. A top 10 hit in Europe, it only reaches #35 in the U.S. On the same day, rehearsals start for Elvis' next Las Vegas engagement.

Live a Little, Love a Little

This movie is a departure from the standard Elvis film of the period. It had a more mature tone with strong language, drug references, and an implied sexual encounter.

Director	Norman Taurog Al Shenberg (assistant)
Producer	Douglas Laurence
Written by	Michael A. Hoey
Based on	*Kiss My Firm But Pliant Lips* by Dan Greenburg
Starring	Elvis Presley Michele Carey Rudy Vallee
Music by	Billy Strange
Cinematography	Fred J. Koenekamp
Editing by	John McSweeney, Jr.
Distributed by	Metro-Goldwyn-Mayer
Release date	October 23, 1968

From dawn to darkroom... from doll to doll... ELVIS clicks with the chicks as a playboy photographer who leads a double-life!

ELVIS PRESLEY shows you how to LIVE A LITTLE LOVE A LITTLE

Elvis in Live a Little, Love a Little, *1968*

Elvis with Rudy Vallee in Live a Little, Love a Little *directed by Norman Taurog [Metro-Goldwyn-Meyer], 1968*

1970 (cont.)

August 10–September 7: Elvis returns to Las Vegas and the International Hotel. MGM shoots a documentary during the engagement that is called *Elvis—That's the Way It Is*.

August 14: Patricia Ann Parker, a Los Angeles waitress, files a paternity suit against Elvis Presley. Elvis is served papers at the Forum arena in Los Angeles on November 14. He countersues on December 16. The law suit drags on for some years; a blood test is not conclusive.

August 28: Elvis is plagued by death threats. He and his entourage carry weapons and the FBI gets involved.

September 7: The final night of his most recent engagement at the International Hotel in Las Vegas, the hotel presents him with the gold belt he'll wear regularly for the rest of his life. It's fashioned to look like a boxing championship belt for his "World Championship Attendance Record" set during his engagements at the hotel.

September 9–14: Elvis' first tour since 1957 starts in front of 13,300 fans at the Veterans Memorial Coliseum in Phoenix, Arizona. The tour will go to St. Louis, Missouri, on the 10th; Detroit, Michigan, on the 11th; Miami, Florida, on the 12th; Tampa, Florida, on the 13th, and Mobile, Alabama, on the 14th.

September 21: Roy Nixon, the sheriff of Memphis, makes Elvis an honorary deputy. Elvis starts to collect police and government badges.

October 1: Produced on RCA's budget label, Elvis' 39th album, *Almost in Love*, is released and will be certified platinum in 2006. Side 1 comprises "Almost in Love," "Long-Legged Girl (with the Short Dress On)," "Edge of Reality," "My Little Friend," and "A Little Less Conversation." Side 2 comprises "Rubberneckin'," "Clean Up Your Own Back Yard," "U.S. Male," "Charro!," and "Stay Away Joe."

Charro!

This Western film represents a lot of firsts for Elvis. It was his only role that didn't feature him singing on-screen and had no songs at all except for the main title theme. Elvis also wore a beard for the first and last time in any of his films.

Director	Charles Marquis Warren George Templeton (assistant)
Producer	Charles Marquis Warren
Written by	Frederick Louis Fox (story) Charles Marquis Warren
Starring	Elvis Presley, Ina Balin, Victor French
Music by	Hugo Montenegro
Cinematography	Ellsworth Fredericks
Editing by	Al Clark
Distributed by	National General Pictures
Release date	March 13, 1969

ON HIS NECK HE WORE THE BRAND OF A KILLER. ON HIS HIP HE WORE VENGEANCE.

A different kind of role...

A different kind of man.

National General Pictures
ELVIS PRESLEY CHARRO!

A bearded Elvis in Charro! *1969*

1971 (cont.)

October 6: "You Don't Have To Say You Love Me" and "Patch It Up" are released. The single reaches #11 on the Top 100 and #1 on the Easy Listening chart. It also reaches #1 in France.

October 19: Elvis and Priscilla create the TCB (Taking Care of Business) jewelry line. The first design is made into 12 gold pendants with the letters TCB and thunderbolts by Schwartz and Ableser Jewelers in Beverly Hills. Later designs will include diamond and gold rings. The jewelry will be given to the Memphis Mafia and other friends and family.

November 4: Another budget album, *Elvis' Christmas Album*, is a re-release of Elvis' original 1957 album. It sells 10 million copies. The tracks are changed and the run time is reduced. Side 1 includes "Blue Christmas," "Silent Night," "White Christmas," "Santa Claus Is Back in Town," and "I'll Be Home for Christmas." Side 2 is "If Every Day Was Like Christmas," "Here Comes Santa Claus (Right Down Santa Claus Lane)," "O Little Town of Bethlehem," "Santa Bring My Baby Back (to Me)," and "Mama Liked the Roses."

November 11: The documentary *Elvis—That's The Way It Is* opens to good reviews. The album of the same name is also released, but only one of the songs, "I Just Can't Help Believin'," is from a stage performance included in the documentary. The other songs are studio recordings. The album reaches #21. Side 1 is " I Just Can't Help Believin'," "Twenty Days and Twenty Nights," "How the Web Was Woven," "Patch It Up," "Mary in the Morning," and "You Don't Have to Say You Love Me." Side 2 is "You've Lost That Lovin' Feelin'," "I've Lost You," "Just Pretend," "Stranger in the Crowd," "The Next Step Is Love," and "Bridge Over Troubled Water."

December 4: Elvis and Priscilla complete the purchase of 144 Monovale in the Holmby Hills neighborhood of Los Angeles for $339,000. After the Manson murders, Elvis wants room for bodyguards and better security. The house is surrounded by a security fence. In 1975 Elvis sold the house to Telly Savalas for $625,000.

The Trouble with Girls

A traveling vaudeville troupe arrives in a small Iowa town in 1927 where internal squabbles create friction within the group. The new manager, played by Elvis, is trying to prevent an actress in the company from recruiting the performers to form a union.

Director	Peter Tewksbury George Templeton
Producer	Lester Welch
Written by	Mauri Grashin
Based on	*The Trouble with Girls* by Dwight V. Babcock and Day Keene
Starring	Elvis Presley Marlyn Mason
Music by	Billy Strange
Cinematography	Jacques R. Marquette
Editing by	Al Clark
Distributed by	MGM
Release date	September 3, 1969

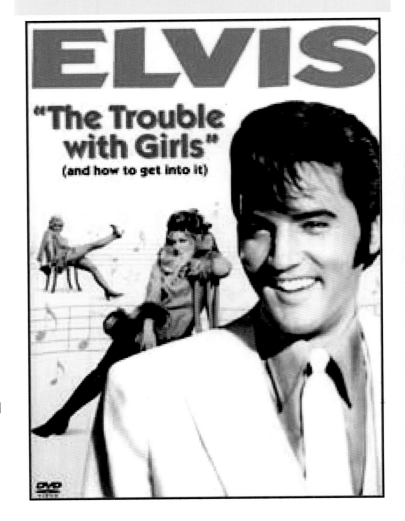

December 8: The single "I Really Don't Want to Know" and "There Goes My Everything" reaches #2 on the Easy Listening chart and makes it to #21 on the Hot 100.

December 19–22: Elvis goes AWOL after Colonel Parker complains that he is being too extravagant and is backed up by Priscilla and his father, Vernon. Elvis meets up with Jerry Schilling in Los Angeles. He takes his police badge collection with him and determines to get a Bureau of Narcotics and Dangerous Drugs badge. He writes to President Richard Nixon who invites him to Washington D.C. where he will meet the president and get his badge. In return, he gives President Nixon a Colt 45 pistol. He is accompanied by Schilling and Red West.

December 28: Elvis is best man at his bodyguard Sonny West's wedding in Memphis.

December 30–31: Elvis returns to Washington D.C. and visits the headquarters of the National Sheriffs Association and tours FBI headquarters, but fails to meet J. Edgar Hoover.

1971

January 2: The 37th Elvis album, *Elvis Country (I'm 10,000 Years Old)* is a huge success reaching #12 in the U.S. and #8 in the U.K. It is certified gold in 1977. Side 1 is "Snowbird," "Tomorrow Never Comes," "Little Cabin on the Hill," "Whole Lotta Shakin' Goin' On," "Funny How Time Slips Away," and "I Really Don't Want to Know." Side 2 is "There Goes My Everything," "It's Your Baby, You Rock It," "Fool," "Faded Love," "I Washed My Hands in Muddy Water," and "Make the World Go Away."

January 9: Elvis is voted One of the Ten Outstanding Young Men of the Nation by the U.S. Junior Chamber of Commerce (The Jaycees). He accepts the award at the Holiday Inn Rivermont in Memphis on January 16 where he delivers a speech.

January 27: Elvis orders female versions of the TCB pendants, entitled TLC, for "Tender Loving Care."

Change of Habit

Elvis, in the role of a physician in a ghetto clinic, falls for a co-worker, played by Mary Tyler Moore, unaware that she is a nun.

Director	William A. Graham
Producer	Joe Connelly
Written by	Eric Bercovici, John Joseph, James Lee, Richard Morris, S.S. Schweitzer
Starring	Elvis Presley, Mary Tyler Moore
Music by	Billy Goldenberg, Buddy Kaye, Ben Weisman
Cinematography	Russell Metty
Editing by	Douglas Stewart
Distributed by	MCA/Universal Pictures
Release date	November 10, 1969

Elvis with Mary Tyler Moore in Change of Habit, *1969*

Elvis and Priscilla, talking to Frank Sinatra, attend Nancy Sinatra's opening night party for her Las Vegas engagement in 1969. Nancy (with her back to the camera) is talking to Fred Astaire.

Elvis Presley in 1969

Elvis with President Richard Nixon on December 21, 1970, in the Oval Office of the White House

1971 (cont.)

January 27–February 23: Elvis plays another long engagement at the International Hotel in Las Vegas, with two shows a night at 10:30 p.m. and midnight.

February 23: "Where Did They Go, Lord?" and "Rags to Riches" are released. The single reaches #33.

March 16: Elvis has eye problems and is diagnosed with secondary glaucoma.

March 22: Elvis' third gospel album, a compilation of songs from as early as 1957, *You'll Never Walk Alone*, is released. It will be certified three-times platinum in 2004. Side 1 is "You'll Never Walk Alone," "Who Am I?" "Let Us Pray," "Peace in the Valley," and "We Call on Him." Side 2 is "I Believe," "It Is No Secret (What God Can Do)," "Sing You Children," and "Take My Hand, Precious Lord."

May 15–21: Elvis heads back to RCA's Nashville studios for another marathon session in which 40 more songs recorded.

May 25: "Life" and "Only Believe" are released—another Easy Listening hit reaching #8 on that chart.

June 16: Not his best work from this period, *Love Letters from Elvis*, is released. Side 1 comprises "Love Letters," "When I'm Over You," "If I Were You," "Got My Mojo Working," and "Heart of Rome." Side 2 comprises "Only Believe," "This Is Our Dance," "Cindy, Cindy," "I'll Never Know," "It Ain't No Big Thing (But It's Growing)," and "Life."

June 22: "I'm Leavin'" and "Heart of Rome" are released. The single reaches #2 on the Easy Listening chart.

June 29: The Memphis City Council votes to change Elvis' home street, Highway 51 South, to Elvis Presley Boulevard. His Tupelo birthplace opens to the public.

July 20–August 2: Elvis plays for two weeks at the Sahara Hotel in Lake Tahoe, Nevada.

Elvis: That's the Way It Is

Documentary of Elvis' Summer Festival in Las Vegas during August 1970.

Director	Denis Sanders
Starring	Elvis Presley
Music by	Joe Guercio
Cinematography	Lucien Ballard
Distributed by	Metro-Goldwyn-Mayer
Release date	November 11, 1970

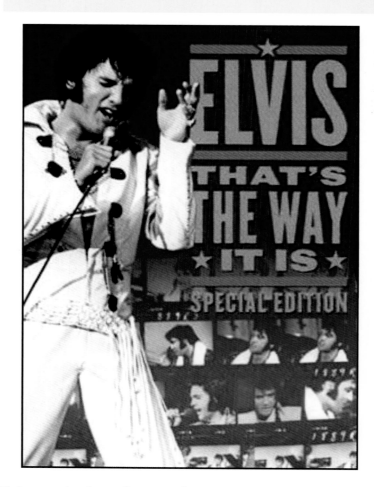

Elvis, wearing his infamous white jumpsuit designed by Bill Belew, in the documentary Elvis: That's the Way It Is, *1970*

1971 (cont.)

August 9–September 6: Elvis plays at the newly renamed Las Vegas Hilton International Hotel. On August 28 he is presented with the Bing Crosby Award from the same organization that presents the Grammys. (The award will later be renamed the Lifetime Achievement Award.)

September 21: "It's Only Love" and "The Sound of Your Cry" are released.

October 6: Another compilation album, *I Got Lucky,* is released. It will be certified gold, and later in 2011, platinum. Side 1 includes "I Got Lucky," "What a Wonderful Life," "I Need Somebody to Lean On," "Yoga Is As Yoga Does," and "Riding the Rainbow." Side 2 includes "Fools Fall in Love," "Love Machine," "Home Is Where the Heart Is," "You Gotta Stop," and "If You Think I Don't Need You."

October 20: Elvis' last Christmas album—*Elvis Sings the Wonderful World of Christmas*—is a huge seller and by 1999 was certified three-times platinum. Side 1 is "O Come All Ye Faithful," "The First Noel," "On a Snowy Christmas Night," "Winter Wonderland," "Wonderful World of Christmas," and "It Won't Seem Like Christmas (without You)." Side 2 is "I'll Be Home on Christmas Day," "If I Get Home on Christmas Day," "Holly Leaves and Christmas Trees," "Merry Christmas Baby," and "Silver Bells."

November 5–12: Elvis goes on a 12-city concert tour with J.D. Sumner. The Stamps Quartet and comedian Jackie Kahane (who will give a eulogy at Elvis' funeral) is the opening act. Elvis wears capes with his jumpsuits and uses a new guitar—a customized Gibson Dove with an Ebony finish, numbered 539461—which will be his staple until September 3, 1973. It has gold keystone tuners, a black Dove-shaped pickguard, a rosewood bridge with dove pearl inlay, a kenpo karate decal, and Elvis' name inlaid on the rosewood fret board. After the November 6 show, announcer Al Dvorin ends by saying "Elvis has left the building," an attempt to convince encore-hungry crowds to go home.

November 9: "Merry Christmas Baby" and "O Come, All Ye Faithful" are released.

Elvis: On Tour

This documentary won a Golden Globe Award. It was Elvis' 33rd and final motion picture.

Director	Robert Abel Pierre Adidge
Producer	Robert Abel
Written by	Robert Abel Pierre Adidge
Starring	Elvis Presley
Music by	Elvis Presley
Cinematography	Robert C. Thomas
Editing by	Ken Zemke
Distributed by	Metro-Goldwyn-Mayer
Release date	1972

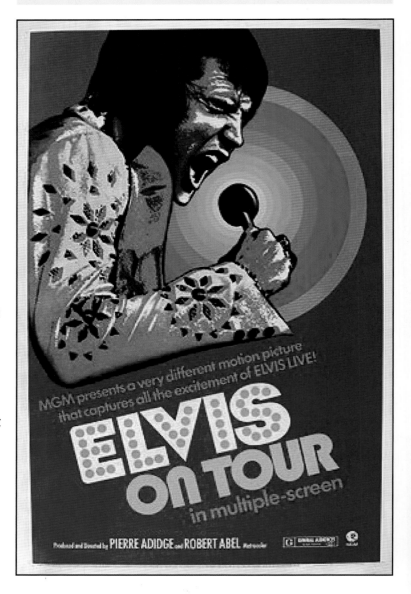

STRUGGLE AND HEARTBREAK

December 31: Elvis tells his entourage that Priscilla will be divorcing him.

1972

January 4: "Until It's Time for You to Go" and "We Can Make the Morning" are released. The single makes it to #5 in the U.K.

January 8: Elvis invites a new girlfriend, Joyce Bova, to join his 37th birthday party in Memphis.

January 26–February 23: Elvis plays another successful engagement at the Hilton in Las Vegas.

February 4: Elvis' latest management contract officially starts, and Colonel Parker gets a third of Elvis' concert proceeds for the next two years.

February 4: "He Touched Me" and "Bosom of Abraham" are released by RCA as the third of seven annual Easter gospel single releases.

February 20: Certified gold in 1992, *Elvis Now*, composed of older material, is released. Side 1 includes "Help Me Make It through the Night," "Miracle of the Rosary," "Hey Jude," "Put Your Hand in the Hand," and "Until It's Time for You to Go." Side 2 includes "We Can Make the Morning," "Early Mornin' Rain," "Sylvia," "Fools Rush In," and "I Was Born about Ten Thousand Years Ago."

March: Colonel Parker and MGM agree to a million dollar deal for a documentary, Elvis on Tour, to be filmed on Elvis' forthcoming concert tour. It will win a 1972 Golden Globe and be his last film.

April 3: Elvis' fourth and last gospel album, *He Touched Me*, wins him his second Grammy Award for Best Inspirational Performance. Side 1 is "He Touched Me," "I've Got Confidence," "Amazing Grace," "Seeing Is Believing," "He Is My Everything," and "Bosom of Abraham." Side 2 is "Evening Prayer," "Lead Me, Guide Me," "Sing You Children," "There Is No God but God," "Thing Called Love," "I John," and "Reach Out to Jesus."

April 4: "An American Trilogy" and "The First Time Ever I Saw Your Face" are released. The single does best in the U.K. where it peaks at #8.

April 5–19: "Elvis on Tour" plays Buffalo, New York, on April 5; Detroit, Michigan, on April 6; Dayton, Ohio, on April 7; Knoxville, Tennessee, on April 8; Hampton Roads, Virginia, on April 9; Richmond, Virginia, on April 10; Roanoke, Virginia, on April 11; Indianapolis, Indiana, on April 12; Charlotte, North Carolina, on April 13; Greensboro, North Carolina, on April 14; Macon, Georgia, on April 15; Jacksonville, Florida, on April 16; Little Rock, Arkansas, on April 17; San Antonio, Texas, on April 18; and Albuquerque, New Mexico, on April 19.

June 6: *Elvis Sings Hits from His Movies, Volume 1*, is released. The first of two volumes, this album was certified platinum in 2004. Side 1 is "Down by the Riverside/When the Saints Go Marching In," "They Remind Me Too Much of You," "Confidence," "Frankie and Johnny," and "Guitar Man." Side 2 is "Long-Legged Girl (with the Short Dress On)," "You Don't Know Me," "How Would You Like to Be?" "Big Boss Man," and "Old MacDonald."

June 9–20: Elvis plays four sell-out shows at Madison Square Garden in New York City on June 9–11 in front of audiences that include rock glitterati such as Bob Dylan, John Lennon, and even Liberace, who suggested Elvis should jazz up his costumes. The tour continues in Fort Wayne, Indiana, on June 12; Evansville, Indiana, on June 13; Milwaukee, Wisconsin, on June 14 and 15; Chicago, Illinois, on June 16 and 17; Fort Worth, Texas, on June 18; Wichita, Kansas, on June 19; and Tulsa, Oklahoma, on June 20.

June 18: Just nine days after recording is completed, RCA releases the taped live album *Elvis: As Recorded at Madison Square Garden*. Side 1 includes "Introduction: Also Sprach Zarathustra," "That's All Right (Mama)," "Proud Mary," " Never Been to Spain," "You Don't Have to Say You Love Me," "You've Lost That Lovin' Feelin'," "Polk Salad Annie," "Love Me," "All Shook Up," "Teddy Bear/Don't Be Cruel," and "Love Me Tender." Side 2 includes "The Impossible Dream," Introduction by Elvis, "Hound Dog," "Suspicious Minds," "For the Good Times," "An American Trilogy," "Funny How Time Slips Away," "I Can't Stop Loving You," "Can't Help Falling in Love," and "End Theme."

Elvis Presley in 1970

Elvis with country singer Dottie West at the Landmark Hotel in Las Vegas on February 25, 1971

Elvis on stage in Las Vegas, 1971

Elvis: Aloha from Hawaii

The concert heard 'round the world on January 14, 1973—except in the U.S. The U.S. audience had to wait until April 4 to see what the rest of the world saw live in January. Elvis performed a vast array of old and recent hits:

"Also Sprach Zarathustra," performed by the Joe Guercio Orchestra

"See See Rider"

"Burning Love"

"Something"

"You Gave Me a Mountain"

"Steamroller Blues"

"My Way"

"Love Me"

"Johnny B. Goode"

"It's Over"

"Blue Suede Shoes"

"I'm So Lonesome I Could Cry"

"I Can't Stop Loving You"

"Hound Dog"

"What Now My Love?"

"Fever"

"Welcome to My World"

"Suspicious Minds"

"I'll Remember You"

"Long Tall Sally"/"Whole Lotta Shakin' Goin' On"

"An American Trilogy"

"A Big Hunk o' Love"

"Can't Help Falling in Love"

The closing vamp was performed by the TCB Band and the Joe Guercio Orchestra. Also accompanying Elvis were J.D. Sumner and the Stamps Quartet, the Sweet Inspirations, and Kathy Westmoreland. After the concert was over, Elvis returned to the empty arena with the TCB Band to record five songs for the American airing of the show, which would not occur until April. The songs included Gordon Lightfoot's "Early Morning Rain" and a couple of songs from the movie Blue Hawaii, "Hawaiian Wedding Song" and "Ku-U-I-Po."

Elvis: Aloha from Hawaii

A cancer benefit concert broadcast live via satellite and taped for U.S. concumption to be aired on April 4, 1973.

Director	Marty Pasetta
Producer	Marty Pasetta
Starring	Elvis Presley
Editing by	Stephen McKeown
Studio	Pasetta Productions
Distributed by	RCA
Release date	January 14, 1973 (Worldwide)

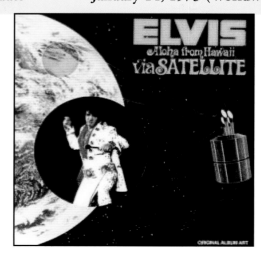

Elvis performing in his concert Aloha from Hawaii on January 14, 1973

1972 (cont.)

July 6: Bill Browder invites Linda Thompson, who at that time was Miss Tennessee, to the Memphian theater on one of Elvis' reserved movie nights. During the show Elvis sits next to her. Shortly after she returns from a two-week vacation with her aunt and uncle, Elvis invites her to go with him to Las Vegas where he is due to start a long engagement. She agrees and a four-year relationship begins.

July 26: Elvis and Priscilla's separation is formalized.

August 1: "Burning Love" and "It's a Matter of Time" are released. The single goes to #3 in Australia, #4 in Canada, #7 in the U.K., and #2 in the U.S. on the Hot 100—a platinum seller.

Elvis performing in Las Vegas

August 4–September 4: Elvis plays at the Hilton in Las Vegas, and Linda Thompson stays with him. On the last night, during a press conference, a major TV concert from Hawaii is announced.

August 15: Priscilla files for divorce from Elvis agreeing to a $100,000 cash settlement plus a $1,500 monthly payment to support her and Lisa Marie. In addition, Priscilla gets a 1971 Mercedes Benz, 1969 Cadillac El Dorado, and a 1971 Harley-Davidson motorcycle, as well as half of the income from the sale of their three houses in California. In October 1973, the actual settlement will differ from this signed agreement.

October 31: "Separate Ways" and "Always on My Mind" reaches #3 on the Easy Listening chart, #20 on the Hot 100, and goes gold.

November 1: Robert Abel and Pierre Adidge's documentary *Elvis on Tour*—his last film—performs well at the box office and shows Elvis in full 1970s swing, with capes and jumpsuits, karate chops and kisses. The same day *Burning Love and Hits from His Movies, Volume 2*, is released. It will be certified two-times platinum in 2004. Side 1 is "Burning Love," "Tender Feeling," "Am I Ready?" "Tonight Is So Right for Love," and "Guadalajara." Side 2 is "It's a Matter of Time," "No More," "Santa Lucia," "We'll Be Together," and "I Love Only One Girl."

November 8–15: The tour continues in Lubbock, Texas, on November 8; Tucson, Arizona, on November 9; El Paso, Texas, on November 10; Oakland, California, on November 11; San Bernardino, California, on November 12 and 13; and Long Beach, California, on November 14 and 15. After this short tour, he and his entourage fly to Honolulu.

November 17–20: After three shows in Hawaii on the 17th and 18th, Elvis gives a press conference on the 20th announcing that the satellite TV show will be a benefit for the Kui Lee Cancer Fund. Kui Lee, an Hawaiian composer, died of cancer while still in his thirties.

December 1: A month after his last compilation album, another is released. *Separate Ways* will go on to sell over 3 million copies worldwide and be certified platinum in 2004. Side 1 is "Separate Ways," "Sentimental Me," "In My Way," "I Met Her Today," and "What Now, What Next, Where To." Side 2 is "Always on My Mind," "I Slipped, I Stumbled, I Fell," "Is It So Strange?" "Forget Me Never," and "Old Shep."

1973

January 9: Elvis arrives in Hawaii and begins rehearsal for his upcoming special. Producer Felton Jarvis arrives the next day.

January 12: An audience for a full rehearsal of the special raises $25,000 for charity from donations at the door.

January 13–14: Elvis' greatest moment? *Elvis: Aloha from Hawaii Via Satellite* from Honolulu's International Convention Center raises over $75,000 for cancer research. It is beamed by satellite to Australia, South Korea, Japan, Thailand, the Philippines, South Vietnam, and other countries. It is seen on a delayed basis in Europe, but Americans have to wait to see it on April 4 on NBC. In all, it will be seen in about 40 countries by an estimated audience of a billion people.

January 26–February 23: Elvis is back at the Las Vegas Hilton.

January 28: *Elvis on Tour* shares Golden Globe victory with the film *Walls of Fire* as best feature documentary of 1972.

February 4: The double album *Aloha from Hawaii Via Satellite* goes to #1 on the Billboard and country charts. It will be certified five-times platinum in 2002. It's Elvis' first #1 album since *Roustabout* in 1965. Five songs recorded after the show will be issued later on the album *Mahalo from Elvis*. Side 1 is "Introduction/Also Sprach Zarathustra," "See See Rider," "Burning Love," "Something," "You Gave Me a Mountain," and "Steamroller Blues." Side 2 is "My Way," "Love Me," "Johnny B. Goode," "It's Over," "Blue Suede Shoes," "I'm So Lonesome I Could Cry," "I Can't Stop Loving You," and "Hound Dog." Side 3 is "What Now My Love?" "Fever," "Welcome to My World," "Suspicious Minds," and Introductions by Elvis. Side 4 is "I'll Remember You," "Long Tall Sally/Whole Lotta Shakin' Goin' On," "An American Trilogy," "Big Hunk O' Love," "Can't Help Falling in Love," and "Closing Vamp."

STRUGGLE AND HEARTBREAK

February 18: Four men climb on stage during a show in Las Vegas. Elvis and bassist Jerry Scheff immobilize the men using karate moves. No charges are filed.

March 1: Colonel Parker sells Elvis' back catalog to RCA for $5.4 million. Elvis and the Colonel split the proceeds 50/50. This means that they will forego future royalties. In addition, the Colonel arranges for Elvis to have a seven-year, 14-album deal with RCA that is worth $3.5 million. The Colonel renegotiates his contract with Elvis into a 50/50 split on all new royalties.

March 4: "Steamroller Blues" and "Fool" are released. The single will peak at #17 on the Top 100.

March 19: Elvis' estranged paternal grandfather, Jesse D. Presley, dies in Louisville, Kentucky, of a heart attack. Elvis had met him many times over the years, but was always reticent about the relationship because he had divorced his grandmother (Jesse's wife), Minne Mae, and had not been close to his father Vernon.

April 4: The Aloha special is aired on U.S. television for the first time and captures over half of the viewing audience—more U.S. households than man's first walk on the moon.

April 22–30: Elvis has concerts in Phoenix, Arizona, on April 22; Anaheim, California, on April 23 and 24; Fresno, California, on April 25 and 26; Portland, Oregon, on April 27; Spokane, Washington, on April 28; Seattle, Washington, on April 29; and Denver, Colorado, on April 30.

May 4–20: Elvis plays the Sahara Hotel in Lake Tahoe, Nevada, but has to cancel shows from May 17 to 20 because he's suffering from pneumonia and pleurisy, which will dog him throughout the rest of the year. He's beginning to put on weight and use drugs.

June 20–July 3: Elvis is back on the road, playing Mobile, Alabama, on June 20; Atlanta, Georgia, on June 21, 29, and 30, and July 3; Uniondale, New York, on June 22 and 23; Pittsburgh, Pennsylvania, on June 24–26; Cincinnati, Ohio,

on June 27; St. Louis, Missouri, on June 28; Nashville, Tennessee, on July 1; and Oklahoma City, Oklahoma, on July 2.

July 16: The album *Elvis* is released. Often called "The Fool Album" it would be certified five-times platinum in 2010. Side 1 includes "Fool," "Where Do I Go from Here?" "Love Me, Love the Life I Lead," "It's Still Here," and "It's Impossible." Side 2 includes "For Lovin' Me," "Padre," "I'll Take You Home Again, Kathleen," "I Will Be True," and "Don't Think Twice, It's All Right."

July 21–25: Recording sessions begin at Stax Studios in Memphis. It is the first time Elvis has recorded in Memphis since 1969.

August 6–September 3: Elvis goes back to the Las Vegas Hilton for another engagement, but this time he receives some poor reviews. After his final concert, Colonel Parker and Elvis clash. Elvis fires Parker, but soon reverses himself and takes Parker back.

September 7: Red West is accused of assaulting one of Elvis' guests outside the Hilton.

September 8: Elvis and Linda Thompson go to Tom Jones' new Las Vegas opening.

September 22: "Raised on Rock" and "For Ol' Times Sake" is released. The single peaks at #17 on the Top 100.

October 9: Priscilla's divorce settlement is finalized. She will receive $14,200 a year in support, $725,000 cash now, half of the sale of the couple's Palm Springs home, and 5% of all new recordings.

October 13: *Raised on Rock* is released and it's another million-copy seller. Side 1 is "Raised on Rock," "Are You Sincere?" "Find Out What's Happening," "I Miss You," and "Girl of Mine." Side 2 is "For Ol' Times Sake," "If You Don't Come Back," "Just a Little Bit," "Sweet Angeline," and "Three Corn Patches."

October 15: Elvis enters Baptist Memorial Hospital in Memphis with pneumonia and hepatitis. By this time he is also addicted to prescription drugs.

Elvis, Priscilla, and Glen Cambell at George Klein's wedding, December 5, 1970; George had been a good friend of Elvis since his high school days.

STRUGGLE AND HEARTBREAK

December 10–16: Elvis returns to Stax where he records 18 songs used on the 1974 albums *Promised Land* **and** *Good Times*.

1974

January 2: The first of four greatest-hits compilations produced under the title, *Elvis: A Legendary Performer*. This is Volume 1 and sells very well, going to two-times platinum in 1999. Side 1 is "That's All Right (Mama)," "I Love You Because," "Heartbreak Hotel," "Excerpt from 'Elvis Sails'," "Don't Be Cruel," "Love Me," and "Tryin' to Get to You." Side 2 is "Love Me Tender," "Peace in the Valley," "Excerpt from 'Elvis Sails'," "A Fool Such as I," "Tonight's All Right for Love," "Are You Lonesome Tonight?" and "Can't Help Falling in Love."

January 8: Elvis Presley Day is declared on his 39th birthday in both the city and county of Memphis, followed by a parade down Elvis Presley Boulevard.

January 11: The single "I've Got a Thing About You Baby" and "Take Good Care of Her" reaches #4 on Billboard's Hot Country chart.

January 26–February 9: Elvis plays the Las Vegas Hilton again.

January 29: Elvis is hospitalized again for drug abuse.

March 1–20: Another tough tour begins with Elvis playing Tulsa, Oklahoma, on March 1; Houston, Texas, on March 3; Monroe, Louisiana, on March 4, 7–8; Auburn, Alabama, on March 5; Montgomery, Alabama, on March 6; Charlotte, North Carolina, on March 8; Roanoke, Virginia, on March 9; Hampton Roads, Virginia, on March 11; Greensboro, North Carolina, on March 13; Murfreesboro, Tennessee, on March 14; Richmond, Virginia, on March 18; and Memphis, Tennessee, on March 16, 17, and 20. From the start, Elvis used a new guitar, an Ebony 1968 Gibson J200. The final gig, at Memphis, is recorded and includes a rendition of "How Great Thou Art" that will win Elvis his third Grammy.

March 20: The album *Good Times* isn't well received when it is released. Side 1 includes "Take Good Care of Her," "Loving Arms," "I Got a Feelin' in My Body," "If That Isn't Love," and "She Wears My Ring." Side 2 includes "I've Got a Thing About You Baby," "My Boy," "Spanish Eyes," "Talk About the Good Times," and "Good Time Charlie's Got the Blues."

May 10: The single "If You Talk in Your Sleep" and "Help Me" peaks at #17 on the Hot 100.

May 10–13: Elvis begins nearly two months of shows in San Bernardino, California, on May 10; Los Angeles, California, on May 11, and Fresno, California, on May 12.

May 16–27: Elvis plays at a sold-out engagement at the Sahara Hotel in Lake Tahoe, Nevada.

May 20: Edward L. Ashley, who has paid to visit Elvis, is refused admittance to Elvis' suite after the Tahoe show and accuses Elvis' bodyguards of beating him. Later he files a huge lawsuit.

May 27: Lisa Marie, aged 5, meets Michael Jackson, aged 11, when Elvis takes her to a Jackson 5 show in Las Vegas.

June 15–June 30: Elvis plays at Fort Worth, Texas, on June 15; Baton Rouge, Louisiana, on June 17; Amarillo, Texas, on June 19; Des Moines, Iowa, on June 20; Cleveland, Ohio, on June 21; Providence, Rhode Island, on June 22; Philadelphia, Pennsylvania, on June 23; Niagara Falls, New York, on June 24; Columbus, Ohio, on June 25; Louisville, Kentucky, on June 26; Bloomington, Indiana, on June 27; Milwaukee, Wisconsin, on June 28; Kansas City, Missouri, on June 29; and Omaha, Nebraska, on June 30.

July 4: Elvis opens a Tennessee Karate Institute. He and Ed Parker perform a demonstration.

July 7: *Elvis: Recorded Live on Stage in Memphis* is released. The album reaches #1 on the country charts and was certified gold in 1999. Side 1 is "See See Rider," "I Got a Woman," "Love Me," "Tryin' to Get to You," the medley "Long Tall Sally/ Whole Lotta Shakin' Goin' On/Your Mama Don't Dance/Flip Flop and Fly/Jailhouse Rock/ Hound Dog," "Why Me Lord?" and "How Great Thou Art." Side 2 is "Blueberry Hill/I Can't Stop Loving You," "Help Me," "American Trilogy," "Let Me Be There," "My Baby Left Me," "Lawdy

STRUGGLE AND HEARTBREAK

Miss Clawdy," "Can't Help Falling in Love, " and "Closing Vamp."

August 19–September 2: Elvis is back at the Hilton in Las Vegas for an engagement. The opening act is completely new and is well reviewed, but on the second night Elvis reverts to his old show.

September 16: Elvis is presented with his Eighth-Degree Black Belt.

September 19: Elvis and Linda Thompson visit her sister-in-law at the Methodist Hospital in Memphis.

September 27–October 14: Elvis is on tour again visiting College Park, Maryland, on September 27; Detroit, Michigan, on September 29 and October 4; South Bend, Indiana, on September 30; St. Paul, Minnesota, on October 2; Indianapolis, Indiana, on October 5; Wichita, Kansas, on October 7; San Antonio, Texas, on October 8; Abilene, Texas, on October 9; and the Sahara Tahoe in Stateline, Nevada, from October 11 to 14. Elvis isn't well. Vernon and Dee have split up, Linda Thompson has moved out, and he's put on weight and is taking drugs.

September 27: "Promised Land" and "It's Midnight" are released. The album reaches #14 on the Hot 100 and #9 in the U.K.

October 13: *Having Fun with Elvis on Stage* consists of two sides of Elvis' stage act without any songs—just chat, repartee, and jokes. Originally produced for sale at his shows, RCA's version was panned by the critics, although it did make #9 on the Top Country Albums chart.

1975

January 4: "My Boy" and "Thinking About You" proved to be a successful single. It reached #10 on Billboard's Hot 100, #14 on the Country chart, and topped the adult contemporary chart.

January 8: Released on Elvis' 40th birthday, *Promised Land* peaked at #47 on the album charts. Side 1 includes "Promised Land," "There's a Honky Tonk Angel (Who'll Take Me Back In)," "Help Me," "Mr. Songman," and "Love Song of the Year." Side 2 includes "It's Midnight," "Your

Love's Been a Long Time Coming," "If You Talk in Your Sleep," "Thinking About You," and "You Asked Me To." Elvis takes to his bed, without visitors, depressed to have reached the ripe old age of 40.

January 10: Colonel Parker arranges for a benefit concert in Jackson, Mississippi, to raise funds for the victims of a tornado the previous day in McComb, Mississippi.

January 20: Elvis puts a deposit of $75,000 on a Boeing 707, which had been owned by Robert Vesco, but the deal will fall through.

January 29: Elvis is admitted into Baptist Memorial Hospital in Memphis with breathing difficulties and a growing addiction to prescription medication. He's given a special diet which, in conjunction with cortisone treatment, makes him gain weight and appear bloated.

February 5: While Elvis is in Baptist Memorial Hospital, Vernon has a heart attack and ends up in the room next door.

February 14: Elvis leaves the hospital. His doctor attempts to restrict his drugs by daily bringing a regulated amount of medication to Graceland.

March 1: "How Great Thou Art" wins the Grammy for Best Inspirational Performance, which is Elvis' third and final Grammy for 14 nominations, one of which was made posthumously. All three Grammy wins have been for his gospel music.

March 10–13: Elvis is back in the studio—RCA's Sunset Boulevard Studio—recording 11 songs that will end up on the album *Today*. This is his last session in a studio. He is accompanied by *Playboy* cover girl (October 1973) Sheila Ryan, who he sees frequently over a two-year period.

March 15: The compilation album *Pure Gold* is released. It will be certified two-times platinum in 1992. Side 1 is "Kentucky Rain," "Fever," "It's Impossible," "Jailhouse Rock," and "Don't Be Cruel." Side 2 is "I Got a Woman," "All Shook Up," "Loving You," "In the Ghetto," and "Love Me Tender."

Elvis on stage, 1972

STRUGGLE AND HEARTBREAK

March 18–April 1: Elvis' next engagement at the Las Vegas Hilton begins.

March 28: Barbra Streisand talks to Elvis about his appearing in *A Star Is Born* and an official offer comes on April 4. Colonel Parker's counter offer, which is sent to Streisand on April 14, is rejected.

April 17: Elvis buys an ex-Delta Airlines Convair 880 jet and renames it the *Lisa Marie*. He will spend over a half million dollars furnishing it.

April 22: "T-R-O-U-B-L-E" and "Mr. Songman" are released and the single peaks at #11 on the Hot Country singles chart.

April 24–May 5: A new tour starts in Macon, Georgia. Bassist Jerry Scheff rejoins the band after two years away. He's shocked by Elvis' appearance. The other tour dates are Tampa, Florida, on April 26; Lakeland, Florida, on April 27; Murfreesboro, Tennessee, on April 29; Atlanta, Georgia, on April 30–May 2; Monroe, Louisiana, on May 3; Lake Charles, Louisiana, on May 4; and Jackson, Mississippi, on May 5. This last concert is to benefit the city of McComb that was devastated by a tornado. It nets $100,000 for victims of the storm.

May 7: The album *Today* is released. Side 1 is "T-R-O-U-B-L-E," "And I Love You So," "Susan When She Tried," "Woman without Love," and "Shake a Hand." Side 2 is "Pieces of My Life," "Fairytale," "I Can Help," "Bringin' It Back," and "Green Green Grass of Home."

May 30–June 10: Elvis is on the road again starting with five sell-out shows in Huntsville, Alabama, on May 30 and June 1, followed by Mobile, Alabama, on June 2; Tuscaloosa, Alabama, on June 3; Houston, Texas, on June 4 and 5; Dallas, Texas, on June 6; Shreveport, Louisiana, on June 7; and Memphis, Tennessee, on June 10.

July 8–24: After a rest of nearly a month, Elvis goes back on the road starting in Oklahoma

City, Oklahoma, on July 8; Cleveland, Ohio, on July 10; Charleston, West Virginia, on July 11 and 12; Niagara Falls, New York, on July 13; Springfield, Massachusetts, on July 14; New Haven, Connecticut, on July 16 and 17; Richfield, Ohio, on July 18; Uniondale, New York, on July 19; Norfolk, Virginia, on July 20; Greensboro, North Carolina, on July 21; and Asheville, North Carolina, on July 22–24. On the last night of the tour he remonstrates with the audience for being unduly quiet and then gives away a diamond ring and throws his Ebony Gibson Dove guitar into the crowd.

July 27: Elvis buys 13 Cadillacs for family, friends, and tour members, as well as Menni Person, a woman who just happened to be shopping for one.

August 18–20: Elvis opens at the Las Vegas Hilton using an early- to mid-1970s Cherry Sunburst Gibson Dove Custom (because he gave away the Ebony Dove on July 24), which he will keep through April 27, 1976. After five shows he is hospitalized until August 30 and has to cancel 36 performances.

September 2: While waiting for the arrival of his Convair 880, he buys a Lockheed JetStar, which he names *Hound Dog II*. It is on display today at Graceland.

September 30: The single "Pieces of My Life" and "Bringin' It Back" peaks at #33 on the Country chart.

November 10: Elvis' Convair 880—named *Lisa Marie*—is delivered. On November 27, pilot Milo High will take him to Las Vegas.

December 1: Another compilation album, *Double Dynamite*, is released. It is a double album and was compiled from four other compilation albums. It was certified platinum in 2004. Side 1 comprises "Burning Love," "I'll Be There," "Fools Fall in Love," "Follow That Dream," and "You'll Never Walk Alone." Side 2 comprises "Flaming Star," "Yellow Rose of Texas/Eyes of Texas," "Old Shep," and "Mama." Side 3 comprises "Rubberneckin'," "U.S. Male," "Frankie

Elvis on tour, August 1972

STRUGGLE AND HEARTBREAK

and Johnny," "If You Think I Don't Need You," and "Easy Come, Easy Go." Side 4 comprises "Separate Ways," "Peace in the Valley," "Big Boss Man," and "It's a Matter of Time."

December 2–15: Elvis makes good on 16 of the canceled shows at the Las Vegas Hilton in Vegas.

December 31: Elvis performs a special New Year's Eve concert at the Silverdome in Pontiac, Michigan. A record 62,500 fans ring in 1976 with Elvis!

1976

January 4: Elvis and his entourage fly to Colorado to spend his 41st birthday on the ski slopes.

January 14: Elvis spends $70,000 on three Cadillacs and two Lincolns for members of his entourage and members of the Denver police department.

January 16: Elvis' latest craze is racquetball, and he builds a 2,100 square foot, two-story court at Graceland. He tentatively agrees to a plan proposed by Joe Esposito and his doctor, Nick, to build a chain of courts.

February 2–8: Elvis spends a week recording at Graceland, for the albums *From Elvis Presley Boulevard, Memphis, Tennessee* and *Moody Blue*.

March 17–22: Elvis starts his first tour for eight months at Johnson City, Tennessee, on March 17–19; Charlotte, North Carolina, on March 20; Cincinnati, Ohio, on March 21; and St. Louis, Missouri, on March 22.

April 21–27: After a break, Elvis continues touring to Kansas City, Missouri, on April 21; Omaha, Nebraska, on April 22; Denver, Colorado, on April 23; San Diego, California, on April 24; Long Beach, California, on April 25; Seattle, Washington, on April 26; and Spokane, Washington, on April 27.

April 30–May 9: Keeping up his hectic schedule, Elvis performs 14 shows at the Sahara Tahoe in Nevada.

May 27–June 6: Elvis continues touring beginning in Bloomington, Indiana, on May 27; Ames, Iowa, on May 28; Oklahoma City, Oklahoma, on May 29; Odessa, Texas, on May 30; Lubbock, Texas, on May 31; Tucson, Arizona, on June 1; El Paso, Texas, on June 2; Fort Worth, Texas, on June 3; and Atlanta, Georgia, on June 4–6. From May 27 through September 8, Elvis uses a Sunburst 1974 Guild F50 jumbo acoustic.

June 16: Elvis' inner circle is beginning to implode and Elvis is not communicating with Colonel Parker. Parker has to write to Elvis to find out what's going on.

June 25–July 5: Another leg of the tour begins in Buffalo, New York, on June 25; Providence, Rhode Island, on June 26; Largo, Maryland, on June 27; Philadelphia, Pennsylvania, on June 28; Richmond, Virginia, on June 29; Greensboro, North Carolina, on June 30; Shreveport, Louisiana, on July 1; Baton Rouge, Louisiana, on July 2; Fort Worth, Texas, on July 3; Tulsa, Oklahoma, on July 4; and Memphis, Tennessee, on July 5—his last concert in his hometown.

July 13: Vernon fires Sonny, Red, and Dave Hebler—the official reason is economics—but they have also been heavy handed in their role as bodyguards. Elvis has a history of firing members of his team when he gets hot ... and rehiring them later. It's possible he intended to do this. They are incensed and are willing participants in the kiss-and-tell book *Elvis: What Happened?* that is ghosted by gossip columnist Steve Dunleavy. Sonny West will later say that the book was written to bring Elvis to his senses and stop his downward spiral.

July 23–August 5: Elvis goes back to the concert circuit, starting in Louisville, Kentucky, on July 23; then going to Charleston, West Virginia, on July 24; Syracuse, New York, on July 25 and 27; Rochester, New York, on July 26; Hartford, Connecticut, on July 28, where Parker tells Elvis that his performances aren't good enough; Springfield, Massachusetts, on July 29; New Haven, Connecticut, on July 30; Hampton Roads, Virginia, on July 31 and August 1; Roanoke, Virginia, on August 2; and finishing at Fayetteville, North Carolina, on August 3–5.

Elvis and Mary Kathleen Selph on June 30, 1972

STRUGGLE AND HEARTBREAK

August 10: Elvis breaks the racquetball chain agreement, firing Joe Esposito and Dr. Nick for making the deal.

August 27–September 8: The next leg of the tour visits San Antonio, Texas, on August 27; Houston, Texas, on August 28 (poor reviews of this show lead Colonel Parker to recall Dr. Nick); Mobile, Alabama, on August 29; Tuscaloosa, Alabama, on August 30; Macon, Georgia, on August 31; Jacksonville, Florida, on September 1; Tampa, Florida, on September 2; St. Petersburg, Florida, on September 3; Lakeland, Florida, on September 4; Jackson, Mississippi, on September 5; Huntsville, Alabama, on September 6; and Pine Bluff, Arkansas, on September 7 and 8.

August 27: Larry Geller, Elvis' hairdresser, rejoins Elvis' entourage after nine years away.

October 5: After hearing that Red West, Sonny West, and Dave Hebler are planning a book, Elvis tries to pay them to halt publication.

October 12: Elvis even calls Red, who tapes the call. Extracts are published on October 26 in the tabloid *The Star*. Elvis is shattered.

October 14–27: Elvis begins another concert tour in which he uses Martin guitars, the same brand he used when he began his professional career and the last brand he would perform with. The model he used until February 14, 1977, was a 1976 D35. The tour visits Chicago, Illinois, on October 14 and 15; Duluth, Minnesota, on October 16; Minneapolis, Minnesota, on October 17; Sioux Falls, South Dakota, on October 18; Madison, Wisconsin, on October 19; South Bend, Indiana, on October 20; Kalamazoo, Michigan, on October 21; Champaign, Illinois, on October 22; Richfield, Ohio, on October 23; Evansville, Indiana, on October 24; Fort Wayne, Indiana, on October 25; Dayton, Ohio, on October 26; and Carbondale, Illinois, on October 27.

October 29–31: Elvis records at Graceland, including his last single, "Way Down."

November 19: George Klein visits Graceland with Miss Tennessee, Terry Alden, but Elvis falls for Alden's younger sister, Ginger.

November 20: The 19-year-old Ginger and Elvis have their first (chaperoned) date to Las Vegas.

November 24–30: Elvis tours in Reno, Nevada, on November 24; Eugene, Oregon, on November 25 and 27; Portland, Oregon, on November 26; San Francisco, California, on November 28 and 29; ending at Anaheim, California, on November 30.

November 29: Ginger Alden arrives in San Francisco to join Elvis on the tour. Linda Thompson is still there, and when she leaves, she leaves for good.

December 2–12: Elvis plays the Hilton in Las Vegas for the last time. On the 10th, Elvis flies Ginger's family out to Las Vegas to watch the show; on the 11th, Priscilla and her parents are in the crowd; on the 12th, televangelist Rex Humbard goes backstage to pray with him. According to Ginger, Elvis asks her to marry him in his room at the Las Vegas Hilton and slips an engagement ring on her finger.

December 27–31: Elvis plays at Wichita, Kansas, on December 27; Dallas, Texas, on December 28; Birmingham, Alabama, on December 29; Atlanta, Georgia, on December 30; ending with a special New Year's Eve concert in Pittsburgh, Pennsylvania.

1977

January 8: Elvis spends his 42nd birthday in Palm Springs, California, with girlfriend Ginger Alden and her sister, Rosemary.

February 1: Elvis and Ginger fly to Los Angeles for Lisa Marie's ninth birthday.

February 12–21: Ginger joins Elvis on tour in Hollywood, Florida, on February 12; West Palm Beach, Florida, on February 13; and St. Petersburg, Florida, on February 14. At this show Elvis gives away his Martin D35. He replaces it with a Martin D28—the same style he used in the 1950s. The tour continues in Orlando, Florida, on February 15; Montgomery, Alabama, on February 16; Savannah, Georgia, on February 17; Columbia, South Carolina, on February 18; Johnson City, Tennessee, on February 19; and Charlotte, North Carolina, on February 20–21.

Elvis and Priscilla leaving Santa Monica California Superior Court after being granted a divorce on October 9, 1973. The couple were married six years and enjoyed an amicable parting.

STRUGGLE AND HEARTBREAK

1977 (cont.)

March 3: Vernon pushes Elvis to sign his will, leaving control of everything to him. Elvis then heads off for a vacation in Hawaii. He gets sand in one of his eyes. He returns home to Graceland on March 12.

March 17: *Welcome to My World* is released and goes platinum in 1983. Side 1 is "Welcome to My World," "Help Me Make It Through the Night," "Release Me," "I Really Don't Want to Know," and "For the Good Times." Side 2 is "Make the World Go Away," "Gentle on My Mind," "I'm So Lonesome I Could Cry," "Your Cheatin' Heart," and "I Can't Stop Loving You."

March 23–30: Elvis tours again beginning in Tempe, Arizona, on March 23; Amarillo, Texas, on March 24; Norman, Oklahoma, on March 25 and 26; Abilene, Texas, on March 27; Austin, Texas, on March 28; and Alexandria, Louisiana, on March 29 and 30.

April 1–5: Elvis is hospitalized in Memphis and four shows in various locations in the South have to be canceled. He returns to Graceland on the 5th. Priscilla and Lisa Marie fly in to visit.

April 13: Elvis goes to Las Vegas with Alicia Kerwin, a 21-year-old bank teller who leaves him because he's "too depressing." While in Las Vegas, he has breathing problems. He recuperates sufficiently to resume touring on April 21.

April 21–May 3: Elvis plays Greensboro, North Carolina, on April 21; Detroit, Michigan, on April 22; Toledo, Ohio, on April 23; Ann Arbor, Michigan, on April 24; Saginaw, Michigan, on April 25; Kalamazoo, Michigan, on April 26; Milwaukee, Wisconsin, on April 27; Green Bay, Wisconsin, on April 28; Duluth, Minnesota, on April 29; St. Paul, Minnesota, on April 30; Chicago, Illinois, on May 1 and 2; and Saginaw, Michigan, on May 3.

May: The tell-all book *Elvis: What Happened?* is serialized in the U.K. It tells a story of drugs, strange spiritualism, and a fascination for guns. Elvis is devastated.

May 20–June 2: Elvis plays more concerts in Knoxville, Tennessee, on May 20; Louisville, Kentucky, on May 21; Largo, Maryland, on May 22; Providence, Rhode Island, on May 23; Augusta, Maine, on May 24; Rochester, New York, on May 25; Binghamton, New York, on May 26 and 27; Philadelphia, Pennsylvania, on May 28; Baltimore, Maryland, on May 29; Jacksonville, Florida, on May 30; Baton Rouge, Louisiana, on May 31; Macon, Georgia, on June 1; and Mobile, Alabama, on June 2.

June 6: "Way Down" and "Pledging My Love"— the two sides to Elvis' last single—are released and the single peaks at #18. After his death, however, it will eventually reach #1 on the U.S. Country chart, in the U.K.—his 17th U.K. #1 hit— and in Ireland.

June 17–26: Elvis' last concert tour is recorded by RCA for a live album and CBS-TV television special, *Elvis in Concert*. Elvis and his entourage play Springfield, Missouri, on June 17; Kansas City, Missouri, on June 18; Omaha, Nebraska, on June 19; Lincoln, Nebraska, on June 20; Rapid City, South Dakota, on June 21; Sioux Falls, South Dakota, June 22; Des Moines, Iowa, on June 23; Madison, Wisconsin, on June 24; Cincinnati, Ohio, on June 25; and on June 26, his last concert—at the Indianapolis Market Square Arena. From 1970 to 1977, Elvis performed 1,094 shows in 130 cities. He was due to tour again from August 17 to 28 in Maine, New York, Connecticut, Kentucky, Virginia, and Tennessee.

June 24: In Madison, Wisconsin, Elvis sees a fight at a gas station, gets out of his car, and assumes a karate stance. When the two assailants and victim see him they forget the fight and ask for photographs.

July 19: The album *Moody Blue* is released. Side 1 is "Unchained Melody," "If You Love Me (Let Me Know)," "Little Darlin'," "He'll Have to Go," and "Let Me Be There." Side 2 is "Way Down," "Pledging My Love," "Moody Blue," "She Thinks I Still Care," and "It's Easy for You." After his death, the album will hit #3, selling more than 2 million copies.

Elvis in concert, 1973

ELVIS HAS LEFT THE BUILDING

August 4: *Elvis: What Happened?* is published in the U.S. It sells slowly at first, rejected by Elvis fans.

August 16: Elvis' last hours highlight his strange lifestyle. First, he returns to Graceland after midnight in his 1973 Stutz Blackhawk having been to the dentist. Then, at 4:00 a.m. he plays racquetball, before singing at the piano. He goes to bed around 5:00 a.m., taking the first of his twice-a-day packet of drugs to help him sleep. He's accompanied by Ginger. Two hours later, unable to sleep, he takes a second packet, and an hour later, a third. At 9:30 a.m. he goes to the bathroom with a book. After 1:30 p.m., Ginger wakes up, notices Elvis isn't in bed, and goes to the bathroom where she finds Elvis dead. She calls for help, and Al Strada and Joe Esposito come to her aid. They call an ambulance. The ambulance takes Elvis to the Baptist Medical Center where he's pronounced dead. Later that afternoon, Vernon announces his son's death to reporters at 4:00 p.m. outside Graceland. Much later, it is announced that he had traces of nine drugs in his blood: Butabarbital, Codeine, Morphine, Pentobarbital, Placidyl, Quaalude, Valium, and Valmid.

August 18: Elvis lies in state at Graceland and 80,000 fans file past his coffin.

August 18: Elvis' funeral service, arranged by J.D. Sumner, is held at Graceland, with 150 people attending, and 75,000 more outside the gates. He is laid to rest in Forest Hill Cemetery alongside his mother.

October 2: Gladys' and Elvis' bodies are moved to Graceland.

October 3: The single "My Way" and "America, the Beautiful" reaches #22 on the Hot 100 chart, #2 on the Billboard Country singles chart, and #9 in the U.K.

October 3: The CBS special *Elvis in Concert* airs. The double album of the same name is also released and reaches #5, selling 1.5 million copies. Side 1 includes Elvis fans' comments/opening riff/"Also Sprach Zarathustra," "See See Rider," "That's All Right (Mama)," "Are You Lonesome Tonight," "Teddy Bear/Don't Be Cruel," Elvis fans' comments, "You Gave Me a Mountain," and "Jailhouse Rock." Side 2 includes Elvis fans' comments, "How Great Thou Art," Elvis fans' comments, "I Really Don't Want to Know," Elvis introducing his father, "Hurt," "Hound Dog," "My Way," "Can't Help Falling in Love," closing riff, and a special message from Elvis' father. Side 3 includes "I Got a Woman/Amen," "Elvis Talks," "Love Me," "If You Love Me (Let Me Know)," "O Sole Mio/It's Now or Never," and "Tryin' to Get to You." Side 4 includes "Hawaiian Wedding Song," "Fairytale," "Little Sister," "Early Mornin' Rain," "What'd I Say," "Johnny B. Goode," and "And I Love You So."

1979

June 16: Vernon Presley dies of a heart attack at the age of 63. He is buried beside his wife and son at Graceland.

1982

June 7: Graceland opens to the public.

1985

Priscilla's autobiography, *Elvis and Me*, tops the bestseller lists.

1986

January 23: Elvis is the first person inducted into the Rock 'n' Roll Hall of Fame.

1987

January 26: Elvis is awarded the first-ever posthumous presentation of the Award of Merit from the American Music Awards.

1993

January 8: An Elvis stamp is released by the U.S. Postal Service. The choice of image is decided by a ballot in which 1.2 million votes were cast. It is the top-selling U.S. commemorative postage stamp of all time. Some fans deliberately misaddress letters so that they will be stamped "Return to Sender."

1994

May 26: In a secret ceremony in the Dominican Republic, Lisa Marie marries Michael Jackson.

1998

Elvis is inducted into the Country Music Hall of Fame.

Muhammed Ali and Elvis, 1973

Elvis on tour in Ames, Iowa, on May 28, 1976

ELVIS HAS LEFT THE BUILDING

2001

July: Presley Place—a 12-unit housing community, the modern equivalent of Lauderdale Courts, where Elvis and his family first lived when they moved to Memphis, and funded by Elvis Presley Charitable Foundation—opens in Memphis.

November 26: Elvis is inducted into the Gospel Hall of Fame.

2002

June: A remix of Elvis' song "A Little Less Conversation" hits #1 on music charts around the world and is the 18th Elvis #1 in the U.K.

September 24: The album *Elvis: 30 #1 Hits* is an instant success and debuts at #1 in 17 countries. It has sold over 8 million copies to date.

2004

Elvis is inducted into the U.K. Music Hall of Fame as part of the inaugural group of artists.

July 5: More than 1,000 radio stations around the world simultaneously play "That's All Right" to commemorate the 50th anniversary of its recording.

2006

March 27: Graceland is named a National Historic Landmark.

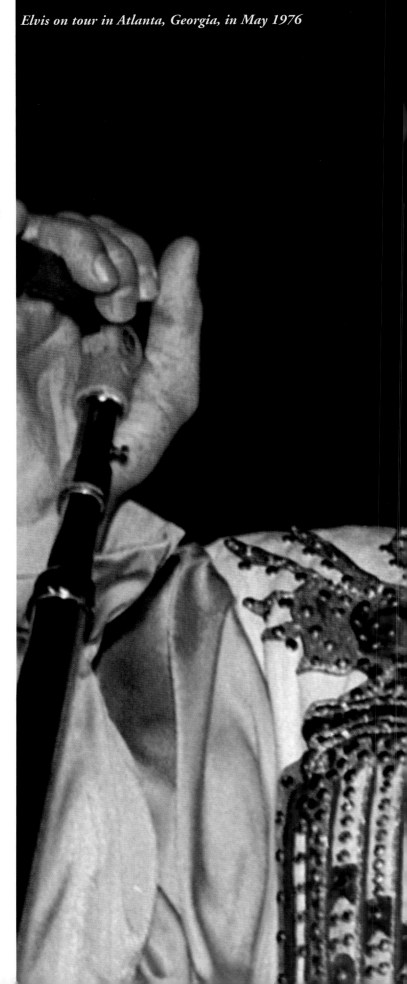

Elvis on tour in Atlanta, Georgia, in May 1976

ELVIS HAS LEFT THE BUILDING

Elvis and his girlfriend of four years, Linda Thompson, (both pictures) returning to the Netherland Hotel after performing in Cinncinati, Ohio, on March 21, 1976. (above)

DEC. 31, 1976
CIVIC ARENA   PITTSBURGH PA
NEW YEAR'S EVE
WITH
ELVIS

Massive crowds (left) turned out to mourn with Lisa Marie, Priscilla, and Vernon at Graceland and along Elvis Presley Boulevard in Memphis. As the caption to the photo on the right states, Lisa Marie and Priscilla are sadly reminiscent of Jackie Kennedy and Caroline at President John F. Kennedy's funeral nearly 15 years earlier. The photo above is especially so.

1977 Blue eyes crying in the rain. Priscilla holds Lisa Marie's hand at her father's funeral August 18th. Priscilla's mother, Ann Beaulieu, is behind the nine-year-old. The shot is chillingly reminiscent of the famous photo of the Kennedy kids at JFK's gravesite

Four views of Graceland in Memphis

Graceland, which had been on the National Register of Historic Places since 1991, was declared a National Historic Landmark on March 28, 2006. Priscilla was there to accept the honor for the family.

A wall of gold and platinum at Graceland, a testament to the Rock 'n' Roll King's unparalleled talent

The interior of Graceland in Memphis and Elvis' piano

Elvis' famous jumpsuit and his guitar on display at Graceland

ELVIS AARON PRESLEY
"The King of Rock 'n' Roll"
WOHNTE WÄHREND SEINER
MILITÄRZEIT
1958–1960
IN BAD NAUHEIM

A memorial to Elvis in Bad Nauheim, Germany, a 30-minute train ride from Frankfurt, Germany. It was in Bad Nauheim on October 1, 1958, that Elvis began his two-year U.S. army service. Here Elvis fell in love with his future wife, Priscilla. Since 2002, Bad Nauheim has hosted the annual European Elvis Festival each August.

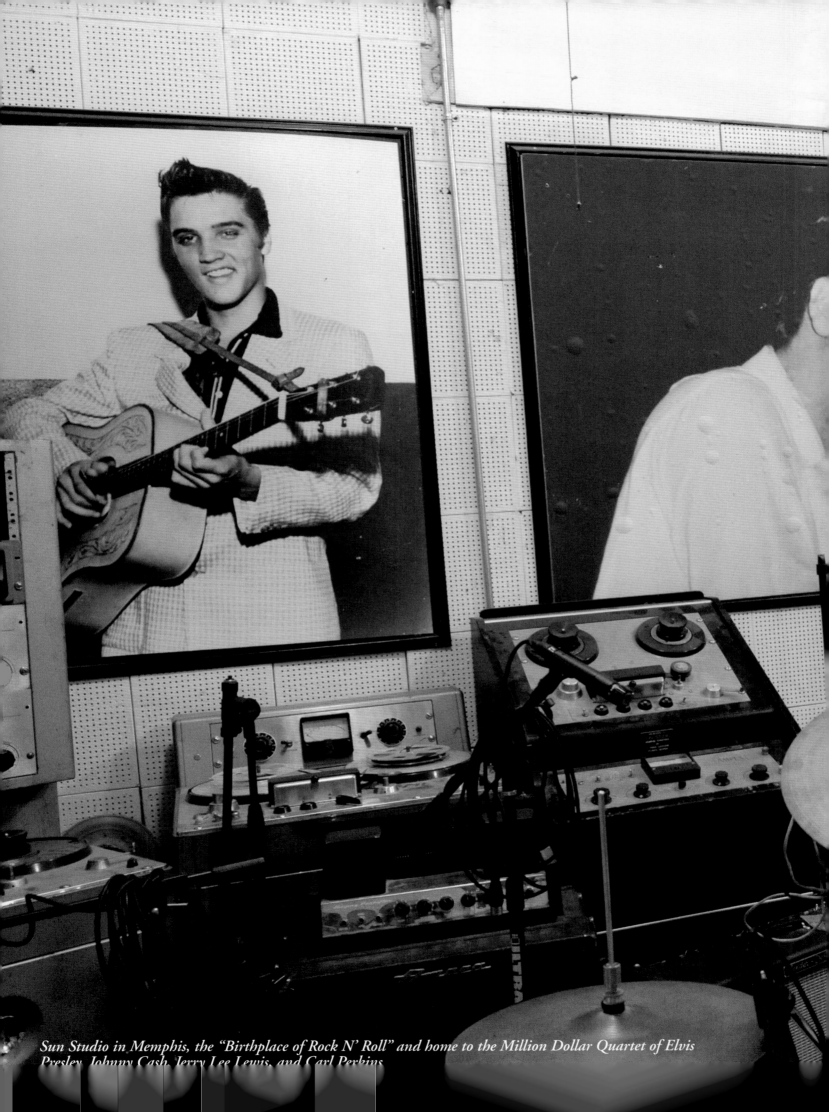

Sun Studio in Memphis, the "Birthplace of Rock N' Roll" and home to the Million Dollar Quartet of Elvis Presley, Johnny Cash, Jerry Lee Lewis, and Carl Perkins.

An Elvis museum in a replica of Graceland in Randers, Denmark

Fans file past the graves of Elvis, his grandmother, and his parents at Graceland in Memphis

Elvis' final resting place in the Meditation Garden at Graceland. Elvis' grandmother, Minnie Mae Presley, and his parents are buried alongside him.

Elvis' Country Music Hall of Fame plaque in Nashville, Tennessee

COUNTRY MUSIC
HALL OF FAME
ELECTED 1998

ELVIS PRESLEY

ARY 8, 1935   AUGUST 16

ORLDWIDE AS THE "KING OF ROCK 'N' ROLL", ELVIS' EARLIES
A COUNTRY MUSIC PERFORMER. AFTER SIGNING HIS FIRS
SUN RECORDS IN 1954, HE RELEASED "THAT'S ALL RIGH
INFLUENCES FROM COUNTRY, GOSPEL AND THE BLUES
ICS DENOUNCED HIS PERFORMANCES AND MUSICAL ST
RE IN MANY MAJOR COUNTRY SHO

The Elvis Museum exhibit at the Imperial Palace in Las Vegas, Nevada

Discography

NUMBER ONE ALBUMS

Year	Album	Type	U.S.	U.S. Country	U.K.
				Chart positions	
1956	Elvis Presley	studio/comp.	1	n.a.	1
	Elvis	studio	1	n.a.	3
1957	Loving You	sound./studio	1	n.a.	1
	Elvis' Christmas Album	studio	1	n.a.	2
1960	Elvis Is Back!	studio	2	n.a.	1
	G.I. Blues	soundtrack	1	n.a.	1
1961	Something for Everybody	studio	1	n.a.	2
	Blue Hawaii	soundtrack	1	n.a.	1
1962	Pot Luck	studio	4	n.a.	1
1964	Roustabout	soundtrack	1	—	12
1969	From Elvis in Memphis	studio	13	2	1
1973	Aloha from Hawaii Via Satellite	live	1	1	11
1974	Elvis: A Legendary Performer Volume 1	compilation	43	1	20
1975	Promised Land	studio	47	1	21
1976	From Elvis Presley Boulevard, Memphis, TN	studio	41	1	29
1977	Elvis' 40 Greatest	compilation	—	—	1
	Moody Blue	studio/live	3	1	3
	Elvis in Concert	live	5	1	13
2002	ELV1S: 30 No. 1 Hits	compilation	1	1	1
2007	Elvis the King	compilation	—	—	1

NUMBER ONE SINGLES

Year	Single	U.S.	U.S. Country	U.K.
			Chart positions	
1956	"I Forgot to Remember to Forget" (reissue	—	1	—
	"Heartbreak Hotel"	1	1	2
	"I Want You, I Need You, I Love You"	1	1	14
	"Don't Be Cruel"	1	1	2
	"Hound Dog"	1	1	2
	"Love Me Tender"	1	3	11
1957	"Too Much"	1	3	6
	"All Shook Up"	1	1	1
	"(Let Me Be Your) Teddy Bear"	1	1	3
	"Jailhouse Rock"	1	1	1
1958	"Don't"	1	2	2
	"Hard Headed Woman"	1	2	2
1959	"One Night"/"I Got Stung"	4	24	1
	"A Fool Such as I"/"I Need Your Love Tonight"	2	—	1
	"A Big Hunk o' Love"	1	—	4
1960	"Stuck on You"	1	27	3
	"It's Now or Never"	1	—	1
	"Are You Lonesome Tonight?"	1	22	1
1961	"Wooden Heart"	—	—	1
	"Surrender"	1	—	1
	"(Marie's the Name) His Latest Flame"/"Little Sister"	4	—	1
1962	"Can't Help Falling in Love"/"Rock-A-Hula Baby"	2	—	1
	"Good Luck Charm"	1	—	1
	"She's Not You"	5	—	1
	"Return to Sender"	2	—	1
1963	"(You're The) Devil in Disguise"	3	—	1
1965	"Crying in the Chapel"	3	—	1
1969	"Suspicious Minds"	1	—	2
1970	"The Wonder of You"	9	37	1
1977	"Moody Blue"	31	1	6
	"Way Down"	18	1	1
1981	"Guitar Man" (remix)	28	1	43
2002	"A Little Less Conversation" (JXL remix)	50	—	1
2005	"Jailhouse Rock" (reissue)	—	—	1
	"One Night"/"I Got Stung" (reissue)	—	—	1
	"It's Now or Never" (reissue)	—	—	1